About the Author

This book is part of a series of publications by Margaret Stacey. As a result of general demands for improved driver behaviour, the original concept was to design an interrelated series of books for all levels of driver and driving instructor.

The first book in the series was *The Driving Instructor's Handbook* written by Nigel Stacey and John Miller, with contributions from Margaret. Since Nigel's death in 1987 Margaret has continued with the co-authorship of this book. Since 1989 it has been recommended by the Driving Standards Agency as essential reading for those studying for the Approved Driving Instructor's Examination.

The second book in the series is *Learn to Drive in 10 Easy Stages* which was first published in 1987 and has now been extensively updated to relate to the latest editions of *The Highway Code* and *Your Driving Test*. This book is recommended to learner drivers by instructors for in-between lesson studies and guidance for those accompanying them during private practice sessions. Margaret also supplies progress/appointment cards to use in conjunction with this book.

The Advanced Driver's Handbook was also published in 1987 and has been selling consistently since that time. This book is designed to improve the skills of those who have a real interest in their driving.

As a direct result of feedback from the driving instruction industry a new publication entitled *Practical Teaching Skills for Driving Instructors* was written by Margaret, together with John Miller and Tony Scriven. This book is becoming widely used by trainee and experienced driving instructors through-out the UK.

Margaret operates a driving instructor training establishment in Derbyshire and publishes her own 'Driving Instructor Home Study Programme' for those studying for the ADI Part 1 Test of Theory. She also produces visual teaching systems to help those involved with driver training at all levels and other stationery materials for driving schools.

Margaret is involved with several ADI organisations at national level. She holds the City & Guilds' Further Education Teacher's Certificate and also certificates in driving from The Institute of Advanced Motorists (IAM), The Royal Society for the Prevention of Accidents (RoSPA), and has also passed the Special Cardington Driving Test for instructors.

For further information Margaret can be contacted at:

The Mount
53 Heanor Road
Ilkeston
Derbyshire DE7 8DY
(Tel/Fax) 0115 932 4499

SECOND EDITION

THE
ADVANCED
DRIVER'S
HANDBOOK

MARGARET STACEY

Illustrated by Andy Rice

KOGAN
PAGE

First published in 1988
Reprinted 1988, 1989, 1990, 1991, 1992
This edition published in 1995
Reprinted in 1996

Kogan Page Limited
120 Pentonville Road
London N1 9JN

© Margaret Stacey and Andrew Rice, 1988, 1995

British Library Cataloguing in Publication Data

A CIP record for this book is available from the British Library.

ISBN 0 7494 1501 0

Typeset by DP Photosetting, Aylesbury, Bucks
Printed and bound in Great Britain by Biddles Ltd, Guildford and King's Lynn

Contents

Foreword

I welcome the arrival of this new edition of *The Advanced Driver's Handbook* –
a well written and informative publication, which every driver regardless of age
and experience would be well advised to study.

There are two groups of drivers who need help, although many within these
groups are either not prepared to admit, or are unaware they have shortcom-
ings. First, the new driver who is embarking on the difficult and dangerous
stage of gaining experience; second, the seasoned driver who has acquired bad
habits and is not up-to-date with the changing circumstances which have called
for improvements and modifications in road procedure.

The author of this handbook, Margaret Stacey, has written a number of
books to assist drivers and driving instructors, and is herself actively involved
with teaching driving and training driving instructors. With John Miller she
wrote *The Driving Instructor's Handbook*, which is recommended by the Driving
Standard Agency as one of the publications for study whilst training to become
a qualified instructor (ADI).

The *Advanced Driver's Handbook* is of particular interest to the College of
Driver Education (CODE) as it complements the objectives of the College and
will fill a long felt want. The College is playing a very important part in the drive
towards greater road safety by helping to reduce road casualties. They offer
assessments with a no pass/fail element to all drivers, ranging from the newly
qualified to the one who has been on the road for anything up to 60 years plus.
For those who enrol for this there are many concessions available including
reduced insurance.

Until now there have been very few publications available to those who may
not be up to the required standard of driving and, we feel that *The Advanced
Driver's Handbook* will provide the help needed. We hope that every driver,
however seasoned and self-satisfied, will become aware of its existence and
study it.

Elwyn Reed MBE
Chairman
College of Driver Education

Introduction

In 1993, there were approximately 229,100 personal injury accidents on British roads. This figure was accompanied by a decrease of one per cent in the volume of traffic and includes all classes of road user.

The statistics showed that there was an increase of one per cent in casualties among car drivers and passengers resulting in a total of 187,100 injuries. Car driver and passenger fatalities totalled 1,740.

You may think you are much safer on the roads these days because of:

- the lower speed limits being enforced in an increasing number of urban areas;
- traffic calming measures;
- improved vehicle design with many new safety features to protect car passengers and pedestrians;
- more efficient braking and anti-lock braking systems;
- anti-skid road surfaces near crossings and at accident black spots.

In the first quarter of 1994 road deaths increased again. There is therefore absolutely no place for complacency, and you may have to think seriously about changing the style of your driving and your attitude towards it.

Can you imagine the amount of grief and suffering which is caused to those who lose a close relative or friend through a road traffic accident? The families of those who may have caused a death will also have suffered a great deal!

It is not only the personal emotional upheavals which we should be aware of. The cost of one accident alone is astronomical in terms of:

- expenses of ambulance, fire and police service involvement;
- costs to the National Health Service when this money could have been used on other patients;
- lost income caused through time off work where serious injuries are involved;
- repair/replacement costs;
- court costs where driving offences have been proved;
- the embarrassment of seeing your name in the local newspaper;
- the overall effects of disqualification and maybe imprisonment.

Driver behaviour is probably the biggest factor leading to most accidents and behaviour is often the result of:

- lack of skill;
- lack of knowledge;
- inexperience;
- unsafe attitudes;
- impairment.

This book is written to help you recognise where accidents are most likely to happen, predict what others are likely to do, and take defensive action to avoid conflict with other road users. It is also designed to help you use your car more sympathetically so that your running costs are minimised.

Do not be misled into thinking that 'advanced driving' means 'fast driving'. On the contrary – it means driving smoothly with skill, efficiency and applying defensive techniques which will enable you to protect yourself, your passengers and other road users around you.

Even if you are an experienced driver, there may be room for some improvement. Answer these questions honestly to see if you need to update yourself and perhaps adapt your style of driving to suit today's cars and the road and traffic conditions:

- Do you think you are an up-to-date, good driver?
- How long ago did you pass your driving test?
- Can you still read a number plate at 20.5 metres (67 feet)?
- Do you sometimes see road signs or markings and wonder what they mean?
- When did you last read the Highway Code?
- Do you have a Highway Code and is it the latest edition?
- Have your children or friends been taught to drive differently from the way in which you were taught?
- Do you think about the comfort of your passengers when you're driving?
- Do you sometimes get to your destination feeling wound up or frustrated?
- Are you getting the best performance and economy from your car?
- Since passing your test, have you ever considered having your driving assessed?

No matter what the standard of your driving is, or what experience you may have, this book is designed to show you how you can improve your skills. Hopefully, by the time you reach the last page, you will have learnt something – you may even have started putting some of it into practice. I certainly hope it will help you to enjoy your driving more!

1 Why Road Accidents Happen

This section describes the causes of accidents and suggests ways in which you can improve your own performance and avoid conflict with other road users.

The causes of road accidents

With the improvement of vehicle design and reliability, statistics now show that vehicle defect is only a very minor cause of accidents. The major defects which contribute to about 8 per cent of the total number of road accidents are:

- tyres, brakes, steering, lights, mechanical failure, electrical failure, loads, windscreen, bad visibility, overall poor condition and unsuitable design.

Adverse road environment contributes to about 28 per cent of accidents and includes:

- adverse road design:
  - unsuitable layout or junction design;
  - poor visibility due to layout;
- adverse environment:
  - slippery road or flooded surface;
  - lack of maintenance;
  - weather conditions or dazzle;
- inadequate street furniture or markings:
  - inadequate signs;
  - worn road markings;
  - street lighting;
  - badly sited signs obscured by trees, etc.;
- obstructions:
  - road works;
  - parked vehicles or other objects.

The major cause, which contributes to about 95 per cent of all road accidents, is human error. This includes factors relating to:

- perception:
  - lack of concentration;
  - failure to see or recognise the risk;
  - failure to correctly judge speed or distance;
- lack of skill:
  - inexperience;
  - lack of good car control skills;
  - lack of judgement;
  - incorrect actions or decisions;
- the way in which actions are taken:
  - excessive speed;
  - unsafe overtaking;

- failure to look properly;
- following too closely;
- irresponsible, reckless, frustrated or aggressive behaviour;
- impairment:
  - alcohol;
  - drugs;
  - fatigue;
  - illness;
  - emotional stress.

Because of the extremely high proportion of human error resulting in the majority of road accidents, this book concentrates on driver behaviour and how to improve your skills and performance.

Factors influencing driver behaviour

In the past it has been suggested that advanced driving is based on altruism. This would imply that safe drivers always consider the rights and safety of others. Although this is an extremely desirable quality, the behaviour of the human being is seldom governed by these motives. It is more likely to be true that good drivers take responsibility for preserving their own safety.

As a good driver, you should always be considering the actions and potential actions of other road users and be prepared to compensate for their mistakes. You should be in the correct frame of mind for driving, be physically well and be able to see clearly, with glasses if worn. Set out on journeys, no matter how short, allowing plenty of time for possible holdups. Keep your car in good condition so that you get the maximum performance out of it. Plan well ahead and allow time for hazards to clear, using the controls of your car gently and smoothly.

Aggressive drivers

We seem to be living in a fast-moving world where people have to get from A to B as quickly as possible and with very little regard for anyone who may get in the way.

Many drivers seem to have a total disregard for the law as far as speed limits are concerned, and they consider that the driver who keeps within the law is a 'Wally'.

There are very few nowadays who class driving as a skill and courtesy seems to be a thing of the past.

Unfortunately aggression on the roads seems to be becoming the norm rather than the exception, and among many young drivers this is even more apparent. Often, when young drivers have several of their peers in the car, it seems to be important to:

- show off by not wearing a seatbelt;
- take off at speed in order to throw your passengers about;
- consistently break the speed limits;
- constantly push even the smallest car to its limits;
- swap and change lanes to the left and right to get ahead of the queue;
- force other drivers to wait, even when it is their priority;
- show absolutely no consideration for pedestrians;
- brake harshly at the last moment for hazards;
- the ultimate, of course, is to go 'joyriding' – or is it 'deathriding'!

Sometimes 'professional' drivers fall into the 'aggressive' category. 'Reps' are often put under pressure to get to their appointments as quickly as possible. The pressure then increases should there be any holdups in the traffic. A large percentage of this type of driver breaks the speed limits and drives too closely to the vehicle ahead as part of their normal driving pattern.

Timid drivers

The timid driver can be just as hazardous as the aggressive one in today's volume of traffic. Drivers who are timid may often, unwittingly, encourage other drivers to take risks by overtaking in the wrong places. They move away too slowly and may not drive up to higher speeds which are safe for the conditions.

Timidity is very often a direct result of insufficient training, especially in car control skills. This means that instead of becoming really familiar with the car, and learning how to handle it reasonably well and with some confidence, they are forced into difficult situations where there are too many things to think about.

Unless confidence is built up from day one, it is highly probable that the timid driver will never enjoy motoring and often be the unwitting, and sometimes unknowing, cause of an accident.

Inexperience

Lack of experience is another major factor in the cause of accidents. Most people opt to take a minimum number of driving lessons prior to taking their driving test. This is, of course, human nature wanting to invest the minimum amount of time and money into obtaining what is considered to be everyone's 'right' – a driving licence.

Driving instructors, because of these commercial pressures, often have to let their principles take second place and pander to these whims by training people to a basic standard in order to 'scrape' through the test.

As road users, we would all be far better off if all new drivers, and the parents of the younger ones, took the view that they were taking out an insurance premium for their future, and learned 'safe driving for life' (which is the Driving Standards Agency's motto). This means that a proper syllabus, and not just the basic content of the current driving test, is covered.

With just a few more lessons, hazard awareness and anticipation skills in a wider variety of situations could be developed to a higher standard. There would then be less likelihood of having an accident during those first few years on the road.

When they have only just passed the test, many people do not get sufficient opportunities to drive often enough to build up their confidence. When they do get the chance to drive, they may not realise that their skills could have deteriorated.

Most people learn to drive in small to medium-sized cars. After passing the test the driver is entitled to drive cars of all sizes and with no restrictions on power. Some, unfortunately, are allowed to drive vehicles with far too much power and response than they are ready to deal with.

Attitude

Attitudes are formed by a combination of a person's experiences and their own individual personality. They are reflected by the way in which people respond to others and how they deal with different situations and problems. Judgements are usually made as a result of how someone personally perceives situations in relation to their own experience. This may not always be in tune with things as they actually are or how others may perceive them. Because of motivational or emotional influences a driver's attitude can suddenly change from one of consideration to that of outright hostility.

Drivers with selfish attitudes expect everyone else to give way to them and show very little, if any, consideration for other road users. This selfishness has resulted in many changes over recent years. The introduction of pelican crossings probably resulted from too many accidents occurring because drivers were reluctant to stop at zebra crossings.

The problem of selfish attitudes and speed appears to be worsening, particularly in our urban areas. As a result of this we are advised to 'Kill your speed – not a child!'

Many councils are now introducing traffic calming measures – some of which are very severe and restrict the width of the road so that only one vehicle at a time can pass through.

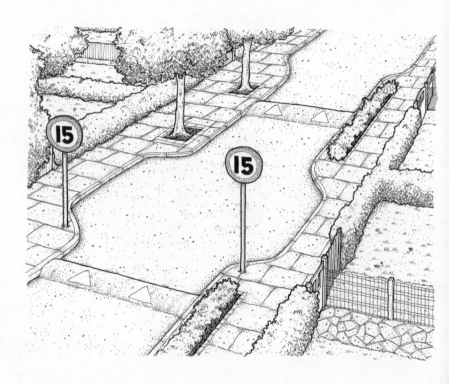

Motivation

This word describes your personal needs and drives. Motivation in the human being is usually directed to survival, well-being and achieving fulfilment of personal desires. It can sometimes affect drivers in unusual ways, for example a driver may be influenced into taking risks which might otherwise have been totally unacceptable if:

- late for work or an important appointment;
- provoked into trying to get revenge on the driver who just overtook;
- trying to demonstrate a superiority of skill and/or gain the admiration of the opposite sex or peers;
- trying to satisfy one's own ego.

Before setting out, allow yourself plenty of time for your journey and say to yourself: 'I am going to do my best to drive smoothly and enjoy this trip.'

Emotion

This word describes how you feel and can relate to feelings such as love, hate, fear, respect, etc. Emotions such as anger, frustration or grief can sometimes be so intense that they can totally distract your mind from what is happening all around. Such a distraction could be caused by something as simple as having an argument with someone close. This could in turn lower your attention on the driving task, severely limit your perception and result in careless errors.

Being late for an appointment can cause so much frustration if you also become held up behind a slow moving vehicle, that you take what otherwise would have been an unacceptable risk and overtake before you know it is completely safe.

Before you drive, it is suggested that you take a few moments to relax, try to clear your mind and get into the mood for driving.

Personality

Everyone is an individual. Your personality is formed by a combination of the characteristics you inherited together with your life's experiences. The way in which we see ourselves is not always the same as others see us. We sometimes outwardly display a different personality from the one we really feel inside.

The fact that extrovert drivers are more likely to be involved in road accidents than those with introvert personalities may be linked to an inability to concentrate for long periods of time. Or it may simply be more difficult to try to work out what we think others expect us to do, instead of doing what we think is correct.

If you have a good knowledge of the correct driving procedures, and the skills to carry them out, you should try to react safely to any situation as you perceive it. This may be more effective than trying to work out what you think your passenger wants you to do. This can often happen when drivers take an advanced driving test. They see a situation developing and instead of responding immediately, ponder on what the 'examiner' is thinking – this distraction often results in the situation ahead worsening, leaving the driver with very little time to deal with it.

Knowledge

It is assumed that knowledge influences attitudes and helps in the acquisition of driving skills.

Make sure you are fully up to date with the latest Highway Code rules and regulations, and be aware of the critical events which can lead to accidents. This should help you recognise risks, respond to them earlier and avoid conflict with other road users.

Physical and mental impairment

Driving is a skill which requires full concentration for one hundred per cent of the time. However, we are all human! High levels of concentration cannot be sustained for long periods. It is even more difficult to concentrate if you are feeling a little under the weather, have been under some kind of stress or are taking drugs.

Extreme emotions such as fear or anger can affect:

- your attention levels;
- your perception;
- your response to everyday situations;
- your ability to reason quickly and logically.

Driving is, in itself, a stressful activity. High levels of frustration can be created by:

- the vehicle;
- the traffic environment;
- the weather conditions; and
- other drivers.

Increased stress can result in over-reaction which may make an already awkward situation even more stressful.

In the case of inexperienced drivers, over-reaction may be caused by:

- lack of confidence in awkward situations; resulting from
- deficiencies in basic car control skills.

These problems are caused because inexperienced drivers are being faced with new situations with which they cannot cope. Not only have they got to think about coping with what is happening on the road, but they are also still worrying about controlling the car.

Aggression

Aggression on our roads is becoming more common as the pace of modern life increases. It is sometimes linked to an individual's desire to dominate others.

Aggression is often displayed by selfishness and open hostility. It may be a way in which the aggressor is trying to compensate for personal feelings of inadequacy or inferiority.

Fortunately, most drivers are able to tolerate a degree of aggression towards themselves without retaliating. However, it is unlikely that aggression can be completely suppressed. The aggressive driver needs educating in the full consequences of selfish driving.

Young people are generally more at risk of showing aggression as they have not yet had enough experience or learnt how to control their emotions. However, aggressive behaviour is not restricted to any particular age group or gender if drivers are pushed beyond their limits.

Illness

Everyone suffers, from time to time, from temporary illnesses such as colds, toothache, headache or tummy upsets.

Remember, these conditions may reduce your attention, impair your vision, or cloud your judgement, timing and co-ordination. Make allowances and if you are taking any non-prescribed drugs, read the labels carefully.

If you have any major illness, or one of a more permanent nature, check whether you need to inform the Driver and Vehicle Licensing Authority at Swansea.

Ageing

None of us are immune to the effects of nature! As we grow older we become more set in our ways and reluctant to adapt to change. Reactions slow down, the memory becomes less sharp, and perception and co-ordination skills may become impaired.

Your health and eyesight may deteriorate. Make sure that you still comply with the legal requirements. Have your eyesight checked at least every two years. If you need glasses for driving, make sure you wear them every time you go out in the car!

As you grow older make allowances for your slower reactions by reading the road further ahead so that you have more time to anticipate possible events and to make your decisions in good time.

Fatigue

This is normally a temporary condition, but it can affect the ability of all drivers. It may:

- reduce your ability to concentrate;
- impair your vision and other senses;
- slow down your reactions;
- make decisions more difficult;
- make you more irritable and less tolerant of others.

It can be caused by:

- overwork;
- emotional stress;
- driving for too long with no breaks;
- boredom;
- illness;
- over-eating;
- too much heat/lack of ventilation in the car;
- bright sunlight or constant glare from oncoming headlights;
- carbon monoxide poisoning.

To avoid problems of fatigue:

- try to delay your journey if you have been overworking or are suffering from stress;
- take frequent breaks during long journeys, and if there is more than one driver in the car take turns at the wheel;
- if you become bored, try listening to some light entertainment;
- if you feel really unwell, avoid driving if possible;
- try to avoid eating large meals prior to driving;
- keep your car well ventilated;
- if you are constantly dazzled try taking a break;
- keep your car in good condition – if the exhaust system has a leak carbon monoxide may be seeping into the passenger compartment. Make sure boot seals are effective and that tailgates of estate cars or hatchbacks are fully closed. Carbon monoxide is colourless, odourless, tasteless – and poisonous!

Alcohol and drugs

The Highway Code states that you must not drive under the influence of drink or drugs.

Alcohol

Since the first barrel of ale was brewed and whiskey distilled, drinking has become a social activity. However, since the invention of the motor car many deaths have been caused by drink-related accidents. It is imperative that we reduce this toll to an absolute minimum.

Alcohol is a drug which is a contributory factor in over 30 per cent of road accidents. After just one drink a driver becomes less able to make decisions and react promptly. After a second drink the driver will become more relaxed, showing less concern for normal restraint and attention to detail. Mental responses and physical reactions will deteriorate and there will be a degeneration in co-ordination and manipulative skills.

After a third drink, emotions become more extreme and behaviour exaggerated. The driver will become more confident and talkative or alternatively morose and sullen. There will be a further deterioration in reactions and co-ordination and perceptive responses will become slower. Impossible feats are likely to be attempted as confidence increases.

Following a fourth and fifth drink there is still a further deterioration in co-ordination to the point of clumsiness. Confidence continues to increase whilst perceptive skills are unknowingly decreasing. Levels of attention and powers of discrimination and restraint are rapidly disappearing as the perception of moving and static objects becomes blurred. Impossible feats are even more likely to be attempted as the driver's ability to make sensible decisions and react promptly become totally unreliable. At this point it is likely that manoeuvres involving a high degree of risk will be unwittingly attempted. Sometimes these end in tragedy!

Over the past few years drink-drive campaigns have fortunately resulted in a decrease in drink-related accidents. However, recent legislation has been introduced whereby some traffic offences result in more serious penalties.

Think, before you drink, before you drive! Is that drink worth losing your driving licence for?

Drugs

Drugs, like alcohol, can affect driving ability by reducing:

- your attention levels;
- your perception of risk;
- your ability to make safe decisions quickly;
- your ability to respond promptly to the changing road and traffic scene.

Studies in the USA show that about 10 per cent of drivers involved in accidents take non-alcoholic drugs of some kind. If you are suffering from any illness you should ask your doctor whether the drugs being prescribed will affect your driving. If you buy any non-prescribed drugs from the chemist or other outlet, make sure you read the label carefully. Many common remedies can cause drowsiness.

Amphetamines are a type of drug which speeds up the nervous system and is often taken to help the user to 'keep going'. Whilst taking the drug, users may feel more alert and confident. However, when the effect wears off, they are likely to feel very tired and depressed.

Barbiturates are taken to help calm the nerves. They have an effect similar to that of alcohol. However, when the effect wears off, depression may follow. Tranquillisers are often used by people with nervous and emotional conditions. They cause drowsiness and when combined with alcohol can have severe or even fatal consequences.

Marijuana is a hallucinogenic drug. It can act as either a stimulant or depressant. It slows down mental responses and physical reactions, affects the judgement of time and space, and limits the ability of the user to concentrate on more than one thing at a time.

You should be able to work out for yourself the dangers involved if you drive whilst taking drugs!

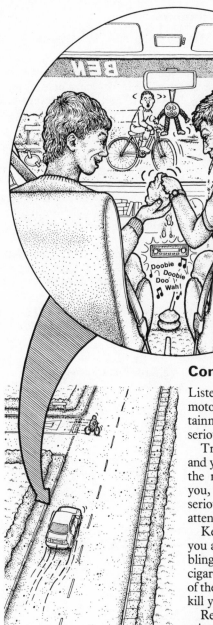

Concentrate and stay alive

Listening to the radio can be useful for motoring reports or a little light entertainment to keep you alert. However, serious listening can be a distraction.

Traffic situations can change rapidly and your attention should be focused on the road. If passengers are talking to you, don't look at them and try to avoid serious conversation as it can lower your attention and slow down your reactions.

Keep your hands on the wheel unless you are operating other controls. Fumbling about for lighters or dropped cigarettes could result in losing control of the car. Smoking whilst driving might kill you sooner than expected!

Remember, if you use a telephone or microphone, you should be stationary. Avoid changing tapes and tuning in the radio when driving, especially at high speed.

Temporary physical distractions

In the Highway Code you are advised to exercise proper control of your vehicle at all times.

- You should not use a hand-held telephone or microphone whilst you are driving. Find a safe place to stop and then use it. You must not stop on the hard shoulder of a motorway to answer or make a call, except in an emergency. Do not speak into a hands-free microphone if it will take your mind off the road.
- Lighting cigarettes can seriously distract you, particularly if you drop either the lighter or the cigarette while you are on the move. Smoking while driving is dangerous as it is likely to affect your control of the steering wheel while changing gear or operating other controls.
- Tuning the radio in, or changing tapes or CDs, whilst driving at speed are open invitations for trouble. As well as affecting your steering, these activities can also seriously distract your attention from the traffic situation.
- If you are travelling to an unfamiliar destination, prepare your plan in advance and have the road numbers and names jotted down and placed where you can see them at a glance. Reading maps and notes while driving is not to be recommended.
- Serious conversation can distract your attention from what is happening on the road ahead and to the rear. If you are talking to passengers, keep your eyes on the road!

It only takes a moment's distraction from the traffic situation to miss a vital warning that you need to slow down or take some other form of action!

2 Understanding Road Accidents

This section explains the importance of being fit to drive and how you can take positive steps to avoid accidents.

Are you fit to drive?

Are you aware of the legal requirements regarding your eyesight? You should be able to read a number plate from a distance of 20.5 metres (67 feet). How long is it since you had your eyes tested?

If you have to wear glasses to see a number plate at the required distance, you must use them for driving. If the number plate appears blurred, how can you expect to read road signs properly?

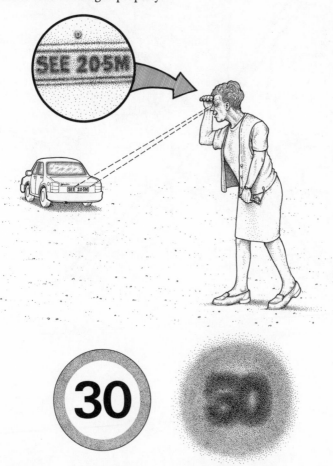

Drinking, drugs and driving

If you are taking any medicines, read the labels carefully. Make sure they do not have any side-effects such as causing drowsiness.

Remember, alcohol is a major cause of accidents – do not drive if you have been drinking. Alcohol may remain in your system for up to twenty-four hours. If you have been drinking heavily the night before you drive, you may still be over the legal limit in the morning!

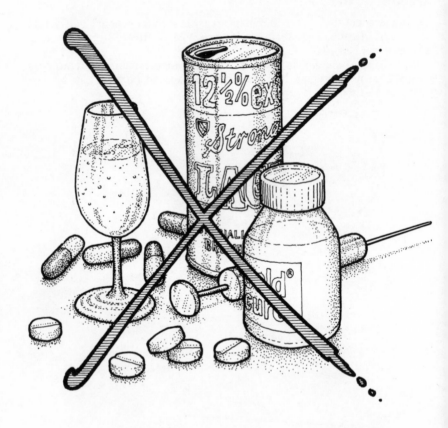

Reduce distractions when driving

Before you drive, particularly if you are going on a long journey, it's a good idea to visit the toilet. If nature calls while you are driving, it will cause a distraction and affect your concentration.

Try to avoid arguments before or during driving. They will put you in the wrong frame of mind and may make you aggressive towards others, as well as taking your attention from the road.

Help yourself to stay alert

Wear light, comfortable clothes. Cars these days have efficient heating and ventilation systems. You shouldn't really need to wear an overcoat – these can often restrict your steering and body movement.

Wear sensible shoes which give you maximum control. Heavy boots or fashion shoes with very high heels are normally unsuitable and may make control jerky. Trainers are extremely popular but beware – the ridges across the soles can sometimes catch on the edge of the pedals making control difficult and sometimes dangerous.

Getting into the car safely

Opening a car door carelessly can put you, your passengers or other road users in danger. Make sure it is safe, open your door and get in as quickly as possible, ensuring that the car is secure by checking the handbrake is firmly on and the gear lever in neutral. It is safer for passengers, particularly children, to get in from the footpath side of the car. Make sure that they open their doors safely with regard for passers-by or other drivers. Listen to make sure all the doors have been closed properly and confirm this by looking down the side of the car for a smooth body line in the mirrors.

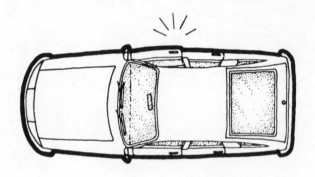

Encourage your passengers to wear seatbelts – it is the law! If you have children in the car and they are under fourteen years of age, their safety is your responsibility. Carry them in the rear unless you have an appropriate restraint in the front passenger seat for any child under three. Never carry children in the back compartment of hatchbacks or estate cars without proper seats. Use the child safety locks and keep children under control at all times. If you have to take animals in your car, make sure they are restrained.

Getting comfortable

Make sure your seating position suits you – if you're uncomfortable you may start getting aches and pains and this will affect your concentration. Adjust your seat so that when you press the clutch down fully, there is a slight bend in your knee.

Sitting too close may result in erratic steering. Sit well back in the seat and, with your hands at the 'ten to two' or 'quarter to three' position, your arms should

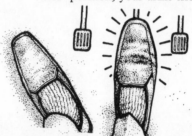

have a slight bend at the elbow. Position your right foot so that you can pivot between the accelerator and brake pedals. If you're driving an automatic keep your left foot well away from the pedals.

Adjust the mirrors so that you can see clearly to the rear and sides with the minimum of head movement. Line up the top edge of the interior mirror with the top edge of the rear window, and the right edge of the mirror with the offside of it. Ask your passengers to sit where they won't restrict your view in the mirrors.

Adjust the door mirrors to reduce the blind areas to the sides of your car to an absolute minimum. If you have extra blind spot mirrors, make sure they are positioned correctly so that they cover the areas you can't see in the other mirrors.

Make sure you can see through the windscreen clearly. The Highway Code states that 'Windscreens and windows must be free from obstruction to vision, and must be kept clean.'

If you're driving an unfamiliar car get used to the position and 'feel' of the controls before moving away.

Concentrating for long periods can be tiring. You will need plenty of fresh air circulating to stay alert. Keep the temperature comfortable but not too warm as this could make you drowsy. Unless you have air-conditioning, a slightly open window will help keep the air circulating and also prevent condensation in cold weather.

Avoiding distractions when driving

If anything in the car moves around while you are driving, it will distract your attention from the road and cause you to have an accident.

Before driving away, look around for any loose articles. Tidy up maps, papers and any other items which may be in danger of moving while you are driving.

Make sure there is nothing on the floor which could roll around – such as a golf ball. As well as being a distraction, if something rolls under the pedals, you may not be able to control them.

Instrument checks

Ignoring warning lights in your car can result in breakdowns or serious damage.

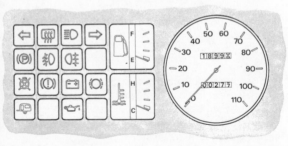

Check that the battery charging and oil pressure warning lights come on when you switch on the electrical circuit, and that they go out when you start the engine.

When you are driving along, to check your instruments just glance at one at a time when there is little happening in the road ahead. If any problems arise with the braking, lubricating or cooling systems, stop as soon as it is safe and, if necessary, get help.

Reducing the risk of breakdowns

Many vehicles involved in accidents have a defect which is either completely or partly responsible for it.

Make sure you keep your car properly maintained according to the manufacturer's handbook. Not only will this reduce your risk of having a breakdown or becoming involved in an accident, but it will also minimise your running costs.

Strict checks are made on cars which have been registered for more than three years. Make sure that your vehicle is up to the standard of the MOT Test. This will reduce the chances of it failing or of you being prosecuted.

Looking through scratched or dirty windows is not only tiring but it can cause glare from either the sun or the lights of oncoming vehicles. Glare is not only painful but it can also cause momentary blindness.

Use water and a soft cloth or leather to regularly clean the windows, mirrors and lights.

Before taking your car onto the road, walk around it looking for any obvious defects. Check that the tyres are properly inflated and that the indicators and lights are working. When you start the engine check that no warning lights remain on and that you have sufficient fuel. If the tank is below a quarter full, it is advisable to top it up as soon as possible. Soon after moving away, test that the brakes are in working order.

On a weekly basis check the oil, water coolant and washer levels, and that the tyres are legal. There should be at least 1.6 mm of tread across the centre three-quarters of the width.

Check the manufacturer's handbook for the servicing intervals – your car will last longer if you look after it properly!

Planning your journey

A large percentage of drivers involved in collisions are within a short distance of home when the accident occurs. There could be a variety of reasons which contribute to this phenomenon.

- Concentration may be at a low level because they:
  - are late for work;
  - had an argument before setting out;
  - are tired after a hard day at work;
  - are frustrated because of a traffic holdup;
  - are worrying about the situation at work or home;
  - are thinking about what they will do that evening;
  - are worrying about family problems, etc.
- There is often a false sense of security in familiar surroundings.

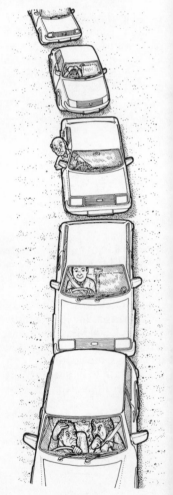

Wherever you are going, whatever time of the day it is, try to concentrate on your driving. Do not let your familiarity with the local environment lull you into a false sense of security. No matter how familiar you are with a road, you can never be sure what will be around that next bend.

Plan long journeys in advance and make a note of your route, jotting down any road and motorway exit numbers. A route card only takes a few minutes to prepare and avoids the need for reading maps while driving.

Have you ever noticed that when something goes wrong, everything seems to go wrong? The later you become, the more people seem to get in your way, and the more red lights there are. The harder it will be to concentrate and the more likely you will be to take risks.

Set out early, allowing plenty of time for road works and other holdups. This will make it easier to concentrate on your driving and avoid frustration and anxiety.

If you do become late, remember it will be far better to arrive late than not at all!

The causes of accidents

An accident is defined as: 'an event without cause'. However, over 90 per cent of road accidents do have a cause – human error!

They often happen because drivers do not expect anything to happen or they simply make false assumptions. Drivers who assume nothing will happen, tend not to consider the 'unexpected', even if it is to some degree predictable. By assuming, they frequently put themselves and other road users at risk. The word 'assume' broken down can be read as making an 'Ass' out of 'U' and 'Me'.

Most serious accidents happen within a five-mile radius of home. This may be due to:

- most journeys taking place within this area;
- over-familiarity with the local roads and 'usual' situations;
- concentration being particularly low at the beginning and/or end of a journey.

Understanding the causes of accidents and anticipating unexpected events by increasing your hazard awareness should help you avoid any conflict with others.

Could you prevent the potential for an accident in this situation?

The most common hazard on our roads these days is parked cars, especially in urban areas. Most families these days own at least one car. Many have two or three vehicles. Unfortunately not everyone has the space to park off the road. Some people have driveways but do not use them!

The potential for accidents is greatly increased where there are lots of parked cars. They:

- obscure vision;
- block junctions; and
- reduce the width of the road (and sometimes the pavement).

The picture below shows one of the most common causes of accidents – a car parked opposite a junction.

There are three possible causes of an accident in this situation.

1. The most obvious problem is the vehicle parked opposite the junction. Drivers who park near junctions are totally selfish. Even if they know the rules, they probably do not realise the risk being caused to their own car, let alone the potential danger into which they are putting other drivers.

   At the end of your journey park safely – well away from any junction. Even if you live near a junction try to consider the safety of other road users as well as your vehicle – not just your own convenience.
2. The driver emerging from the side road is only looking to his right for approaching vehicles. Not having checked to the left, he is totally unaware that a car is pulling over to his side of the road to pass the parked car.

Whatever type of junction you are emerging from, make sure your observations are effective by looking all around for other traffic and obstructions before you decide to pull out.

3. The driver moving out to pass the parked car has 'assumed' that anyone approaching the junction on the right would give way. Having failed to predict the possibility of someone emerging, he/she is travelling too fast to be able to pull up in time to avoid a collision.

Even if there are signs and markings in a side road, never assume that other drivers will obey them. Expect someone to emerge and reduce your speed accordingly so that you can stop safely if necessary.

Be patient

How well do you understand the rules of the road and how courteous are you? Remember, just because you are experienced not everyone else is. If you are planning well ahead and anticipating what is happening you should be able to work out what other drivers are going to do.

Remember there will be drivers who are far less capable than you! Be tolerant and allow for their mistakes or indecisiveness. If you become aggressive it may make the situation even worse and could push the other driver into making a wrong decision. This in turn may result in an accident which could also involve you.

If someone shows aggression towards you, ignore it. Keep calm and let them wait until you are sure it will be safe to go.

The consequences of speed

Too many people drive at speeds which are unsafe for the conditions. This is often because they fail to understand the risks involved.

A 30 mph speed limit is a maximum, but to some it is a minimum which must be maintained regardless of what is happening all around. It is much too fast in areas where there are lots of parked vehicles and a high degree of pedestrian activity.

As a result of drivers ignoring speed restrictions and to increase pedestrian safety, many urban areas now have traffic calming measures and even lower speed limits imposed.

Show consideration to others by driving at speeds which suit the conditions and at which you are able to stop safely within the distance you can see is clear.

If only . . .

Most accidents are preventable.

No matter whose fault or priority it may have been, collisions cause inconvenience, injury, expense and misery to all of those concerned.

Even if you have to give an aggressive driver priority when it is really yours, you will benefit by avoiding conflict.

Accidents take lives. Think before you take a chance. You could hurt someone – or lose your licence, your job, even your life.

3 Hazard Awareness and Planning

This section covers the different tasks involved in dealing safely with the changing road and traffic conditions. It emphasises the importance of planning well ahead, working out what might happen, keeping your options open and having the car under full control all of the time.

Perceptual motor skills

The driving task involves attending, perceiving and responding safely to relevant stimuli. This requires a complex set of interacting perceptive and manipulative skills which are executed partly at a conscious level and partly subconsciously. Together they are the result of the driver:

- obtaining the relevant information from what is happening all around;
- processing the information; and then
- responding by making decisions and carrying out the appropriate car control skills.

Perceptual motor skills include:

- paying attention to the driving task;
- systematically scanning the road and traffic environment;
- identifying and awarding priorities for and to relevant cues;
- assessing the potential risk factors;
- anticipating possible events;
- deciding on the most appropriate action;
- responding in a restrained manner by:
  - communicating with others;
  - changing the speed and/or position of the vehicle in a controlled manner;
  - making further observations and continuously assessing and reassessing the situation.

Paying attention to the driving task

Attention can either be spread over the whole traffic scene or focused selectively on specific areas or objects of particular significance.

Selective attention requires more effort and can only be sustained for short periods. High levels of concentration are difficult for anyone to sustain for more than twenty minutes at a time.

One of the characteristics of good drivers is that they have learnt how to allocate and distribute their attention around in order to maximise any useful information they obtain about the road and traffic hazards.

A hazard is anything containing an element of danger or potential risk which causes you concern or influences you to consider a change to your speed and/ or direction. They include:

- physical features in the environment such as bends, junctions, brows of hills;
- blind areas of road such as dead ground;
- footpaths or relevant nearby areas restricted from view;
- the movement or potential movement of other road users (including pedestrians) into your path;
- the condition of the road surface and any other factors which may affect the stability of your vehicle.

Actual hazards are those which you can see and therefore easily identify. Most drivers are prepared to act when they recognise, for example, a pedestrian running across the road.

Potential hazards, however, are much less easily identifiable and sometimes, because they cannot actually be seen to be happening, are more difficult to accept as being potentially dangerous. This type of hazard includes:

- the potential for movement across your path;
- restrictions to your sightlines near parked vehicles or around bends etc.;
- grit on the road, black ice or other factors affecting stability.

Not only must you recognise the obvious risks of a child actually running into the road, you must also be ready to respond to the child who is standing by the side of the road, and the even less obvious risk of the unseen child who may run out from behind the ice cream van.

Perception is how your brain interprets the information sent to it by your eyes, ears and other senses. It involves comparisons of the current situation with existing knowledge and previous experiences.

Numerous research studies have shown that all drivers have limited perceptual capacities – and yet we are frequently faced with an overload of information from the vehicle, the road and the traffic environment with which we must deal.

Traffic hazards rarely occur in isolation. You often have to attend simultaneously to a number of risk factors in different parts of the road. In these situations you have to make a decision to attend to the most important aspects of the situation and ignore or reject others. You should recognise that this discrepancy between the task demands and your own capabilities does exist but that it can often be reduced by making appropriate reductions in your speed.

Visual search skills

The brain receives 75 per cent of its information from your eyes. Eyes are naturally attracted to movement, bright colours and unusual occurrences. Not all of these are relevant to particular road and traffic situations. You therefore need an effective system of visually scanning to maximise the input of useful information so that you can identify areas of priority. You should:

- look well ahead in order to steer a safe and smooth line;
- make early adjustments to your speed in response to possible hazards, road geometry and traffic signs;
- continually look for situations containing any element of risk, i.e.:
  - the potential for others to move into or across your path;

- areas of restricted vision which may be hiding other road users who could turn into or across your path.

Try to work out in advance what action you will need to take if events change and make an appropriate reduction to your speed.

Anticipation

Driving safely involves anticipating, or predicting, the actions of other road users. The ability to anticipate is closely related to risk assessment and previous experience. Together these are often referred to as hazard recognition skills. Anticipation is also closely related to visual search skills and involves effectively interpreting driving-relevant cues. You should know:

- what to look for;
- what to expect;
- why, where and when you should look more carefully;
- how to look and visually scan the road effectively and assess the potential for danger.

Assessing risk

Driving involves a continuous process of attending to, interpreting and responding to constantly changing needs involving the vehicle, the road layout and the traffic conditions. You have to continually check, assess and reassess hazards and the responses you make to them. You should:

- look, assess and decide on the safest action to be taken from the

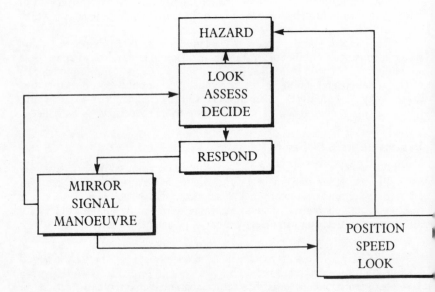

Figure 1 *Driving is a continuous process of assessment and reassessment*

information you have received by looking all around and checking your mirrors;
- look, assess and decide whether or not a signal is required;
- look, assess and decide whether the following driver and other road users are responding to your signal;
- look, assess and decide what effect any changes in your speed and/or position are having or are likely to have on other road users, and decide what further looks may be required, before choosing what action to take.

There is some connection between your own personal assessment of the potential risk in any traffic situation and that of safe driver behaviour. However, your own personal assessment of the risk involved will be influenced by previous experience.

Assessing risks and deciding an appropriate way with which to deal with a traffic hazard involves a continuous chain of checking, rechecking, assessing and reassessing the constantly changing environment. It involves:

- identifying the hazard;
- assessing the degree of risk involved;
- awarding priorities to the hazard in relation to the whole traffic scene;
- directing further attention to the hazard;
- deciding on the safest course of action to be taken;
- responding by:
  - signalling your intentions, and/or
  - maintaining or changing your speed and/or position;
- creating time for the situation to develop and/or obtain additional information before reassessing what to do.

Making decisions

Inadequate information and hurried assessments are a major cause of incorrect decisions. Such decisions often polarise between 'stop' and 'go' when neither are correct. This 'stop – go' method of dealing with hazards is characteristic of those who make decisions which all too often result in a high degree of risk.

Many accidents happen because drivers make their decisions too early. Some drivers are merely indecisive in the first instance and then make a hurried, rash decision on the spur of the moment.

In many instances extra time is needed to allow a situation to develop in order to gather more information before any decision can be safely made. For example, there are three possibilities when approaching a vehicle parked on the left three hundred yards ahead where a line of slow-moving traffic is approaching from the opposite direction. These are:

1. it is safe to proceed past the obstruction at a lower speed;
2. it is definitely unsafe to proceed at the moment;
3. more time is needed to gather more information and assess the situation before a decision to proceed can be made.

A decision to proceed, stop and give way, or hold back must be continually reassessed. For choices 2 and 3 the response, more often than not, will be the same. This will be to delay the manoeuvre, either until safe passage is guaranteed by the circumstances, or until sufficient information has been gathered to make that safe decision. This can be done by:

- slowing down and allowing time for the situation to develop;
- slowing down to obtain more information about the potential movement of any pedestrians nearby;
- gathering more information about the position of oncoming vehicles, or the potential for more oncoming vehicles;
- reviewing the changes in the situation after/and as a result of slowing down;
- improving your view by changing your lateral position and/or 'feeling' your way forward cautiously.

Try to work things out in advance! For example, when approaching a green traffic light, you should anticipate the possibility of it changing and be prepared with a decision to stop. However, at some point on the approach when nearing the stop line, you will obviously be too close to pull up safely. Once you have reached and crossed this point, the only decision you can safely make is to continue.

If you are approaching a red traffic light, anticipate that it may change to green. Check your mirrors to see what is happening behind you, slow down and be prepared either to: change down and accelerate away if they do change; or gradually and smoothly bring your car to a stop at the line.

Whatever colour is showing, you should continually reassess what you will do if the lights change. Your decisions can be made in advance, leaving the response to be triggered by the event – ie the changing light!

Car control skills

Many drivers mistakenly assess the quality of their driving from how well they can handle the car. While car control skills are, of course, extremely important, it is the perceptive and hazard recognition skills which are more significant in the prevention of accidents.

Car control (manipulative) skills involve the ability to:

- communicate with other road users;
- regulate speed;
- steer and position safely;
- maintain adequate safety margins.

After carrying out the look – assess – decide routine and taking a course of action either to proceed, wait or to delay progress until more information has been gathered, you should then respond by putting into practice the normal routine procedures:

- *Mirrors.* Check the mirrors and apply the look–assess–decide routine. Consider how what you have seen may affect your intended manoeuvre.
- *Signal.* The traditional methods of communicating with other road users include direction indicators, arm signals, brake lights, the horn, flashing headlights, hazard warning flashers. However, communication between road users is complex and there are many more ways to 'inform' others.

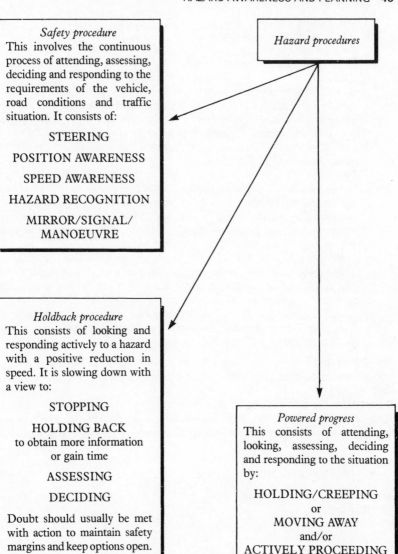

Safety procedure
This involves the continuous process of attending, assessing, deciding and responding to the requirements of the vehicle, road conditions and traffic situation. It consists of:

STEERING

POSITION AWARENESS

SPEED AWARENESS

HAZARD RECOGNITION

MIRROR/SIGNAL/
MANOEUVRE

Hazard procedures

Holdback procedure
This consists of looking and responding actively to a hazard with a positive reduction in speed. It is slowing down with a view to:

STOPPING

HOLDING BACK
to obtain more information
or gain time

ASSESSING

DECIDING

Doubt should usually be met with action to maintain safety margins and keep options open.

Powered progress
This consists of attending, looking, assessing, deciding and responding to the situation by:

HOLDING/CREEPING
or
MOVING AWAY
and/or
ACTIVELY PROCEEDING
in a suitable gear.

Figure 2 *Driving involves assessing and responding correctly to driving-relevant stimuli*

These include:
- the speed of your vehicle;
- the position of your vehicle in the road;
- implied signals of intent - linked to the movement or position of pedestrians;
- making eye contact with others;
- courtesy and acknowledgement signals between road users.

- *Manoeuvre.* The manoeuvre consists of the position–speed–look routine. This can be any event which involves a change in speed and/or direction. It should normally be preceded and followed by the continuous process of looking, assessing and deciding.
  - *Position and speed.* Awareness and your judgement of position and speed should be linked. As you increase your speed, your point of focus should get further ahead and this will be accompanied by a reduction in your peripheral sensitivity (what you can see to your sides). Where there is a need to attend to what is happening in the immediate foreground, there is a corresponding need to reduce your speed.

    Peripheral vision should help you judge your speed and position. A failure to reduce speed at the appropriate times may result in important risk factors going unnoticed, a reduction in awareness of your lateral position, and reduced safety margins.
  - *Look.* The last ingredient of the procedure - but by no means the least! You should now again be assessing, deciding and responding to what you see happening all around.

Try to plan in advance. You should be aware of what is happening at least six vehicles ahead, so that you will be ready to slow down when the cars in front start to brake.

Early planning should make your driving more enjoyable; minimising the need for late and harsh braking. This will also make the ride for you and your passengers smooth, comfortable and safe.

4 Vehicle Handling Techniques

This section describes the different forces which act on vehicles in motion and how you can maintain full control in different circumstances.

Factors which affect the stability of vehicles in motion

Friction provides you with control over the direction and stability of your car. If you exert other forces, which exceed the friction between the tyres and road surface, you will lose control of it.

It is vital that you understand the importance of friction and the other factors which are involved in maintaining stability. These other factors include:

- the adhesive characteristics of your tyres, i.e.:
  - their state of wear;
  - design factors;
  - pressures;
  - mix of radial and crossply;
  - rubber compounds used in their manufacture.
- the grip coefficient of the road surface, i.e.:
  - its state of repair and condition;
  - the type of surface;
  - the presence of lubricants such as water, oil, rubber, mud, grit;
- inertia:
  - the natural phenomenon of a mass to maintain consistent movement unless other forces are exerted on it;
- gravity:
  - the natural force which holds your car on the road and keeps the tyres in contact with its surface. The forces of gravity can be offset by:
  - applying acceleration or braking forces on hills;
  - deflecting your car's direction on roads with severe cambers;
  - driving at speed on curves with adverse cambers.
- the efficiency of the suspension system to cope with the effects of inertia:
  - over uneven surfaces;
  - on bends in the road;
  - when braking, accelerating and cornering;
  - to prevent the tyres becoming airborne.
- the speed of the vehicle:
  - the lift forces being generated.

Partial or complete contact with the road surface may be lost due to:

- a combination of excess speed and an uneven surface;
- an inadequate or faulty suspension system.

Adhesion between the tyres and road surface may be lost due to:

- the tyres riding above the surface on a cushion of water (aquaplaning);

- an excess of oil, rubber or other unstable material on the road;
- excessive acceleration, braking or cornering forces being exerted by the driver. This can cause the rubber compound of the tyre to melt and form a thin film of lubricant on the road surface.

Steering characteristics

Centrifugal and other forces can contribute to the loss of stability of a vehicle when it is being driven on a curved path. The tyres and suspension system are designed to optimise grip on the road surface and control the natural effect of these forces. Steering can be affected by the weight distribution of loads and passengers.

Because of the position of the engine and transmission, front-wheel drive vehicles carry most of the weight at the front. They have a tendency to understeer and have natural stability. Vehicles with the engine and transmission systems at the rear tend to oversteer and are more unstable.

Understeer
This characteristic is built into the design of most modern cars to maximise stability when:

- cornering;
- driving at speed; or
- where there are crosswinds.

Understeer describes the tendency of a vehicle to run wide on a curved path and is compensated for by a slight increase in the degree of steering needed to negotiate a bend safely.

Mild understeer provides good directional stability, placing less demands on the driver. Excessive understeer makes a vehicle more unresponsive and can mean harder work when driving in town where there is a need to deal with lots of 'tight' junctions, or on winding country roads.

Neutral steering or mild oversteer characteristics make the steering more responsive.

Oversteer
This gives less stability, particularly when driving at higher speeds and when cornering. Vehicles with oversteer characteristics are directionally unstable and require frequent correcting, particularly:

- where strong crosswinds are present;
- when driving at higher speed; and
- on roads with pronounced changes in the camber.

Oversteer is the tendency for a vehicle to point itself into a bend more than is anticipated by the driver. It can be compensated for by a decrease in the degree of steering wheel movement.

Over- and understeer characteristics may change as speed is increased. For example, a car which normally understeers can develop neutral steer and then oversteer. To maintain maximum control allow for these changes so that they are progressive and predictable, otherwise they may catch you unaware and prove to be very dangerous.

Changes in accelerator pressure may also affect both over- and understeer. Releasing the accelerator of a front-wheel drive vehicle transfers weight onto the front wheels and increases the cornering force exerted. A vehicle with a tendency towards natural oversteer can snake about quite violently if harsh acceleration is used on a bend or corner.

Slip angles

When steering round a bend, the tyres point in a slightly different direction to the course of the vehicle. It is the difference between the direction of tyre travel and the plane of the wheel which is called the 'slip angle'.

Where the slip angles of the front tyres are greater than those at the rear, the vehicle understeers. Conversely, where the slip angles at the rear are greater than those at the front, it will oversteer.

Radial tyres have smaller slip angles than crossply. It is illegal to fit radial tyres to the front wheels if crossply are fitted to the rear because this creates an oversteer tendency and directional instability.

Roadholding and handling characteristics

There is usually a compromise between the roadholding features built into a vehicle and how it should be handled to give a smooth, safe ride.

The 'ride' describes the smoothed-out motion experienced by passengers as a result of the insulating effect of the tyres, suspension and comfort of the seating.

The 'handling' describes the manner in which the vehicle responds to the driver's use of the accelerator, brakes and steering.

'Roadholding' describes the grip between the tyres and road surface when these forces are being applied to the car.

Due to the weight transfer generated by centrifugal force, the outer wheel on a curve exerts more cornering force than the inside one. This means that a vehicle with negative camber will apply an increased cornering force to the road surface which will reduce its tendency to understeer. Conversely, a vehicle with positive camber will reduce the tendency to oversteer.

Suspension

The purpose of a suspension system is to:

- insulate the vehicle body and its occupants from road shock;
- increase the tyre and road surface adhesion by maintaining contact; and
- improve the roadholding and handling characteristics.

There are various types of springs used in suspension systems. Hydraulic dampers control bounce on bumpy surfaces, and anti-roll bars are fitted to reduce body roll when cornering.

The effectiveness of a suspension system is determined by the stiffness of the springs and the ratio of unsprung weight. A vehicle with excessively hard springing will give an uncomfortable ride and there will be a loss of contact between the tyre and road surface when driven over bumps. This reduces stability and adhesion.

Softer springs with plenty of suspension travel provide a more comfortable ride. Unfortunately, however, this reduces the resistance to body roll when cornering. Excess roll can mean poor handling on corners and soft suspension can result in excessive front-end dip of the car when braking and lift when accelerating.

Aerodynamic instability

Drag increases fuel consumption and holds a car back, particularly at higher speeds. Most cars are now designed aerodynamically by computer to reduce the drag factors and improve fuel consumption. Their shape enables them to slide through the air cleanly, causing little air turbulence.

This can be compared to the shape of aircraft wings which are flat at the bottom so that the air can travel unrestricted directly underneath. The air travelling over the top has to travel further over the curved surface, making it warmer and less dense, while the denser air underneath the wing pushes it up.

As the air passes over a car, it creates a low pressure over the top and produces a lift force. It is worth noting that some four-seater aircraft have take-off speeds of as low as 55 mph!

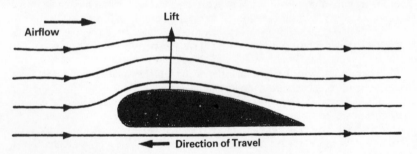

Lift force makes a vehicle lighter and reduces road surface adhesion, particularly at higher speeds. The smoother ride and lighter steering may give the illusion of greater safety. However, don't be lulled into a false sense of security – the vehicle is considerably less stable!

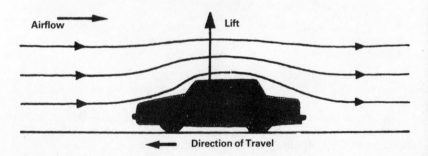

The diagram below shows the forces which act on a vehicle when it is travelling in a straight line and is under light acceleration.

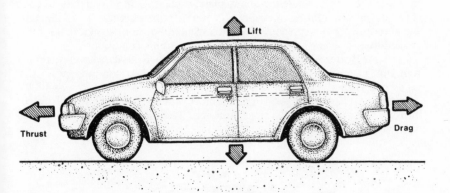

A car passing through an airstream has a 'centre of pressure' through which the aerodynamic forces (lift, drag and crosswind thrust) act. This can be compared with the way in which weight and centrifugal force act through the centre of gravity.

The aerodynamic stability of a vehicle is relevant to the relative positions of the centres of pressure and gravity. If the centre of pressure is ahead of the centre of gravity, the vehicle will become unstable when driven in crosswinds.

Airflow over the body of the car can produce a significant lift force at the front of the vehicle, equivalent to putting additional weight in the boot. This can result in:

- severe oversteer; or
- a reduction in understeer characteristics.

Vehicle instability

Inertia

Inertia is the natural tendency of any mass, such as a car, to maintain its state of rest or uniform motion. Newton's Laws of Motion state that a moving mass will keep moving at a constant speed in a straight line until an external force is applied to it. The car is at its most stable under these conditions.

Inertia will offer resistance to your efforts to change the speed or direction of your car. The effects of inertia can be readily felt when you move off, drive round corners and stop your car.

In order to change the speed or direction of your car, you have to apply forces through the tyre and road surface adhesion. These acceleration, braking and cornering forces reduce stability.

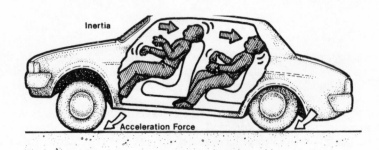

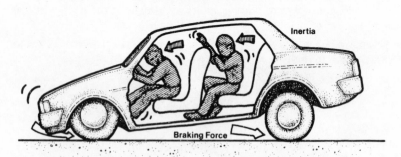

Centrifugal force

This is a natural reaction to, and effect of, *centripetal force*. It is an expression of the resistance offered by inertia to the centripetal (or cornering) force being applied to the vehicle through the adhesion of the tyres to the road surface.

The vehicle wants to continue in a straight line and this inertia will resist the centripetal force applied by the tyres. Newton's Third Law states that the forces occur in equal and opposite pairs. Thus the cornering (centripetal) force of the tyres is equal and opposite to the outward thrust (centrifugal force) of the vehicle on the tyres.

Kinetic energy

There is a degree of energy in any moving body. This is called *kinetic energy*.

In a one-ton vehicle travelling at 60 mph, there is sufficient energy to boil two pints of ice in about four seconds. Kinetic energy is related to the vehicle weight and its speed. Any increase is accompanied by a disproportionate increase in kinetic energy. For example, if you double your speed, the kinetic energy is four times greater.

On a dry road, the braking distance of a car with efficient brakes and good tyres being driven at 40 mph by a skilled driver is about 80 feet (24 metres). If the speed is increased to 80 mph the braking distance is about 320 feet (98 metres), which is four times greater.

At 40 mph the kinetic energy value is over 4,000,000 lb per square foot; at 80 mph it is over 16,000,000 lb per square foot. There is a direct relationship between these figures and the braking distances outlined in the Highway Code. Every time the speed doubles, the braking distance becomes four times greater. For example:

At 20 mph the braking distance is 20 feet (6 metres).
At 40 mph the braking distance is 80 feet (24 metres).
At 80 mph the braking distance is 320 feet (98 metres).

Forces applied to the car by the driver

Unless a car has mechanical defects, it will only go out of control if the driver applies some sort of force which acts in opposition to the prevailing road conditions.

It is not the car which goes out of control – but the driver who loses it!

A moving vehicle is at its most stable when it is:

- travelling in a straight line;
- on a level road;
- at a constant speed.

It will remain stable until an external force is applied.

Driving requires frequent changes in speed and direction. These changes are made by:

- accelerating;
- braking; and
- cornering.

Whenever these forces are applied to the tyres, there is a natural resistance to the changes which makes the vehicle less stable.

Your control over your vehicle relies totally upon the friction between the tyres and road surface. The most important, single factor in maintaining the level of friction between your tyres and the road surface is the way in which you drive your car.

To maintain maximum friction, you must control the effects of inertia by:

- taking corners at appropriate speeds; and
- braking and accelerating smoothly and progressively.

Harsh acceleration, late heavy braking and sudden changes in direction are the hallmarks of bad driving and all too often result in loss of proper control.

Acceleration force is limited by:

- the power of the engine;
- your skill with the accelerator, clutch and gears; and
- the adhesion of the tyres to the road surface.

Instability will occur if you apply too much force too quickly. The resultant resistance to inertia will shift weight from the front to the rear of the vehicle and reduce the efficiency of the steering.

In extreme cases, the natural resistance of the vehicle to acceleration forces may result in the driving wheels skidding on the road surface. You should avoid harsh acceleration and deceleration, particularly in the lower gears or when the road surface is slippery.

Use fifth gear as soon as your car will be 'happy' with it, and when you have reached your cruising speed ease off the gas slightly so that you can maintain the higher speed more economically.

Remember, the natural state of a moving mass is to continue at a constant speed and you will only need more power to overcome the effects of:

- gravity;
- drag;

- tyre rolling resistance; and
- friction losses.

To reduce fuel consumption even further, use your accelerator smoothly, avoiding unnecessary or fidgety movements.

Braking force is limited by:

- the efficiency of the brakes;
- the driver's skill in applying them; and
- the tyre and road surface adhesion.

Engine compression provides a slight braking force when in a high gear and a significantly more pronounced effect when a lower gear is engaged. This means that sometimes it may be appropriate to engage a lower gear for holding back the speed when travelling down a long, steep hill.

Instability occurs when the brakes are used harshly, because the vehicle will resist the forces being applied. The result is a shift in weight from the rear to the front of the vehicle. This makes the steering heavier to handle and reduces the adhesion of the rear tyres on the road surface.

You should look well ahead for signs or obstructions and be prepared to slow down early. Braking in good time for a hazard provides early warning to following drivers. It also permits a gradual reduction in pedal pressure as your car loses speed and creates more time for you to assess the situation and make any necessary gear changes, if you are able to continue without stopping.

To achieve gentle stops there are three phases to the braking process. Keeping both hands on the wheel so that you maintain a straight course:

1. apply an initial light braking pressure;
2. increase the pressure firmly but progressively until the vehicle is pulling up short of the hazard, leaving a margin for error;
3. gradually ease the braking pressure and let the car roll on a little to stop gently in the appropriate position.

This method of stopping reduces the risk of rear-end collisions. It also maximises your passengers' comfort and their confidence in your skills.

A common error when using the brakes is to apply them either too late or too lightly in the intermediate stage. This often results in a harsh, uncontrolled last-minute application and frequent unnecessary stops.

Cornering force is limited by:

- the tyre and road surface adhesion;
- the efficiency of the suspension system; and
- your own skill at steering.

Cornering at too high a speed can cause instability due to the resistance of the centrifugal force to the centripetal force applied by the tyre. The result is a shift in weight to the wheels on the outside of the corner which reduces the adhesion of the inside tyres on the road surface.

The effect of combining cornering with braking and acceleration forces will cause additional imbalance to stability when the tyre adhesion and other factors may be stretched to their limits.

Minimise the need for sudden changes in speed and direction. When your car is subjected to any of these forces, brake and accelerate smoothly, and steer gently keeping both hands on the wheel.

Try to maintain a constant speed on bends and when cornering. Drive at lower speeds in windy conditions and when contact between the tyre and the road surface is reduced in wet or icy weather.

Slow down, or power down, before reaching bends and corners. ('Power down' means easing slightly off the accelerator.) Do this whilst on the straightest course possible. Your approach speed should be low enough to permit you to drive the car round the bend under slight power.

Except when going downhill, use a light pressure on the accelerator to maintain a constant speed. This will help maximise stability. Combinations of harsh acceleration or braking when cornering are to be avoided.

Slow down more than normal on the approach to bends with an adverse camber. Gravity may cause the vehicle to become less stable.

Factors influencing stopping distances

Stopping distances can be affected by:

- your own reactions;
- your state of health;
- the size and weight of your vehicle;
- the effectiveness of its braking system;
- the type of tyres, pressures and depth of tread; and
- the condition of the road surface.

Stopping distances are increased when you are travelling downhill and stopping will take even longer on wet or slippery roads.

If you are fit and alert, on a dry road, in a car with an efficient braking system and good tyres, you should be able to bring it to a stop within the distances shown in Table 4.1 below.

Table 4.1 *Stopping distances*

	Thinking distance			Braking distance			Overall stopping distance	
20 mph	20 ft	(6)	+	20 ft	(6)	=	40 ft	(12)
30 mph	30 ft	(9)	+	45 ft	(14)	=	75 ft	(23)
40 mph	40 ft	(12)	+	80 ft	(24)	=	120 ft	(36)
50 mph	50 ft	(15)	+	125 ft	(38)	=	175 ft	(53)
60 mph	60 ft	(18)	+	180 ft	(55)	=	240 ft	(73)
70 mph	70 ft	(21)	+	245 ft	(75)	=	315 ft	(96)

Note: The figures given in brackets are metres.

When you double your speed, your braking distance is quadrupled.

The common causes of skids and how to correct them

Although, to a degree, the condition of the vehicle and the road surface may contribute to a skid, the main cause is, without any doubt, the driver.

There are three different types of skid and they are caused by either:

- the driver travelling at excessive speeds for the road or traffic conditions;
- the driver applying excessive acceleration, braking and/or cornering forces to the tyres; or
- combinations of both of the above.

You should always be reading the road well ahead and taking into account any changes to the road, weather or traffic conditions. Travel at a speed at which you can maintain full control and use your controls early and gently.

The rear wheel skid

This usually occurs if the rear wheels lose their adhesion with the road surface. It is usually the result of excessive speed and/or cornering forces, possibly in conjunction with harsh acceleration or, more usually, excessive braking.

This type of skid is easily and instantly recognised because the rear of the car slides away from the centre of the corner. Uncorrected, the vehicle may turn completely round.

It is essential to try to eliminate the cause of the skid by releasing the accelerator and/or footbrake and compensate by correcting the steering. As the vehicle will be pointing in the wrong direction, your natural reaction will normally be to steer back on course.

However, over-reacting can sometimes be a danger, particularly with the quick response of radial tyres. Be careful that you don't steer back too far.

The front wheel skid

This may occur if the front wheels lose their grip on the road surface. It can leave you with no control over the vehicle's direction.

The front wheel skid is usually the result of turning sharply into a corner or bend at excessive speed and/or under hard acceleration or braking. It can be easily recognised because the vehicle won't go where you are steering it.

Eliminate the cause and regain steering control by momentarily straightening the wheels and/or by reducing pressure on the accelerator or brake.

The four wheel skid

This occurs when all four wheels lose their grip on the surface. It is usually due to travelling at excessive speeds for the road conditions or traffic situation, resulting in late and uncontrolled overbraking. If the road surface is wet or slippery, you may even feel that your speed is increasing.

This type of skid will leave you with no control over your direction and may result in a combination of turning broadside and your car not responding to your steering corrections.

Control over the steering can be partially restored by momentarily releasing the brake to allow wheel rotation to recover. Then, quickly re-apply the brake in a rapid on–off action.

The prevention of skids is better than the cure!

It is important to recognise danger signs early and act on them before the situation becomes serious. For example, if you see a group of children playing near the road, slowing down early will mean less braking pressure is subsequently needed if one of them dashes out.

Concentration, planning and early anticipation of the possible actions of others is essential. In snow and ice slow down early with light, gradual pressure on the brakes. Gentle braking is less likely to cause skidding than suddenly changing down into a lower gear. Use gradual acceleration and keep in the highest gear possible without distressing the engine. If you are travelling uphill in snow, try to maintain steady momentum while staying well back from the vehicle ahead.

Drive at safe speeds for the road surface conditions. Accelerate, brake and corner gently. Drive more slowly on wet, icy and slippery surfaces. Watch out for loose gravel, fallen leaves and damp patches under trees. Make sure your tyres are correctly inflated and that they have a minimum of 2 mm of tread all around the tyre. Never mix crossply and radial tyres on the same axle.

Here are a few tips which should help you keep full control at all times. Read the surface conditions and remember:

- to slow down well before reaching any bumpy parts of the road or where the edges are rough;
- to keep off soft verges;

- to avoid heavy braking on loose gravel, muddy surfaces and damp patches under trees;
- a combination of oil, rubber dust and water can make the surface very slippery after a light summer shower following a long dry spell;
- in freezing temperatures remember that black ice forms on exposed bridges when the other parts of the road may seem relatively clear.

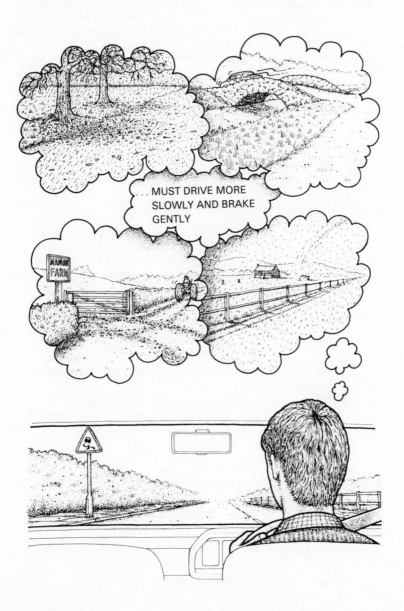

Systems of car control

The natural forces that affect the stability of vehicles in motion are scientific facts. Any system of car control must take these facts into account.

Putting an efficient system of control into practice helps create plenty of time to recognise and assess the road and traffic conditions, and then respond to them correctly and safely.

The system you apply should have a built-in set of safety margins to help you compensate for the mistakes made by other road users, and any minor lapses in concentration which most of us experience from time to time. It will also ensure that you are driving your vehicle sympathetically.

Try to incorporate the following tried and tested principles, into your driving.

- The speed at which you travel should never exceed that at which you will be able to bring your car to a properly controlled stop well within the distance you can see to be clear. You should look for and respond to:
  - any obstructions in your intended course;
  - any potential for other road users to move out of blind areas behind obstructions into or across your intended course;
  - any restrictions to sightlines caused by road features such as bends, hill crests and hollows (dead ground);
  - any potential obstructions which could be hidden by the restrictions to your sightlines.
- The control of your vehicle, and the speed at which you drive, should take into account the forces that affect its stability. You should be aware of:
  - the physical roadholding and handling limitations of your vehicle;
  - the tyre and road surface adhesion and increased stopping distances in wet and icy conditions;
  - the effects of camber and gravity;
  - the aerodynamic forces acting on your vehicle.
- To minimise the effects of the forces affecting your car's stability, you should:
  - apply and remove acceleration, braking and cornering forces smoothly;
  - avoid any excessive acceleration and/or braking forces when negotiating a curved path;
  - avoid changing gear when making major adjustments in your direction;
  - avoid unnecessary gear changes – be selective when changing gear;
  - keep both hands on the steering wheel when accelerating hard, braking and cornering;
  - use gentle, controlled power when negotiating a curved path;
  - use the handbrake if you are stationary for more than a few seconds;
- If you are sympathetic to the needs of your vehicle not only will you prolong its life but also achieve greater economy in the use of fuel. You should:
  - avoid unnecessary or fidgety movements on the accelerator;
  - use the accelerator and/or footbrake early/smoothly;
  - avoid excessive clutch slip, drag and unnecessary coasting;
  - avoid excessive tyre wear by cornering at lower speeds;
  - avoid using gears unnecessarily to reduce speed;

- switch the engine off whilst stationary for prolonged periods;
- delay switching the heating system on before the engine has warmed up;
- avoid using roof signs unless necessary as they cause additional drag;
- avoid carrying unnecessary loads in the boot;
- keep your engine tuned properly;
- check the tyres regularly for uneven wear and pressure;
- have the brakes checked regularly;
- have the vehicle serviced regularly;
- keep a check on the bodywork for corrosion.

Gear-assisted braking

Changing down to reduce speed is unsympathetic on the vehicle, is not normally acceptable as good driving practice, and wastes fuel.

However, on some long downhill gradients, a lower gear may be engaged to offset the effects of gravity. Use the brakes first to bring the speed under control before selecting an appropriate lower gear. This method of 'holding the speed back' provides increased engine braking and reduces the risk of brake failure from overheating.

Selective gear changing

Remember: 'Brakes are for slowing – gears for going!'

If you need to slow down for a hazard which subsequently clears, it is not necessary to change down through every gear. Slow down and then decide on the gear which is most appropriate to the speed and power which you require for moving on again.

Keep both hands on the wheel, use the footbrake to reduce speed and, after slowing down, change down as the hazard clears and accelerate away. For example:

- If there is a parked vehicle on your side of the road and you decide to give way to an oncoming car, keeping both hands on the wheel, leave the gears alone, slow down and hold back to let the other car pass. When it has gone, the gear you select will depend on your speed and how much power your car now needs for pulling away again.
- Approaching the end of a road in third or fourth gear where your sightlines are totally restricted, use the brake to slow down until you have almost stopped. Push the clutch down and gradually ease the braking pressure to let the vehicle roll. Select first gear ready for moving away when you are sure it is safe.

The power change

This technique permits lower gears to be selected smoothly when travelling at higher than normal speeds. It matches the engine speed to the lower gear enabling them to be engaged quickly without the loss of road speed or power. This method of changing gear can be beneficial where extra power is needed for overtaking or climbing a hill.

To change:

- hand on the gear lever and cover the clutch;
- clutch down quickly:
- 'flip' and release the accelerator;
- select the lower gear;
- raise the clutch and accelerate away.

Double de-clutch

This specialised gear changing technique is generally only necessary in some heavy goods vehicles. Although it is still recommended in some advanced driving manuals, it is not very often necessary in modern vehicles which have the gears protected by synchromesh.

To change up:

- hand on gear lever and cover the clutch;
- clutch down and off the accelerator;
- move the gear lever to neutral, clutch up quickly and then down again;
- engage the higher gear;
- raise the clutch and accelerate.

To change down:

- hand on gear lever and cover the clutch;
- clutch down and off the accelerator;
- move the gear lever to neutral;
- clutch up and depress the accelerator quickly – releasing it immediately;
- clutch down quickly and engage the lower gear;
- raise the clutch and continue braking/accelerating.

Heel and toe

This specialised technique is generally only used for high performance driving and is unsuited for normal on-road usage. It permits the driver to make a power change into a lower gear by blipping the accelerator with the heel or side of the right foot whilst braking with the ball of it.

Emergency braking

It may take longer to stop than you think, particularly in wet conditions.
If you have to stop quickly because of unforseen circumstances:

- keep both hands firmly on the wheel to maintain a straight course;
- pivot promptly to the brake and apply it progressively and firmly;
- maximum braking force is applied to the vehicle just before the wheels lock, so avoid braking so hard that the wheels do lock because this will considerably lengthen your stopping distance;
- leave the clutch alone until just before the car comes to a stop. Pushing it down too soon will increase the risk of locking the wheels and also lengthen the stopping distance.

In wet, slippery conditions, if you apply too much pressure on the brakes and lock the wheels, momentarily release the brake to allow the tyres to regain their grip, and then quickly reapply it.

This is sometimes called 'cadence braking'. As the brakes are released and then reapplied some weight is transferred to the front of the vehicle ensuring that the wheels do not lock.

Automatic braking systems (ABS) work in this way, to give the driver greater braking efficiency and increased directional control when, in emergency situations, the driver's natural reaction may be to lock the wheels.

The effects of strong side winds

In high, exposed places, expect strong winds, particularly from the sides. Hold the wheel firmly and be ready to compensate for any deflection when passing high-sided vehicles or after driving over or under bridges. Remember, others at your sides may also be affected, so give plenty of clearance.

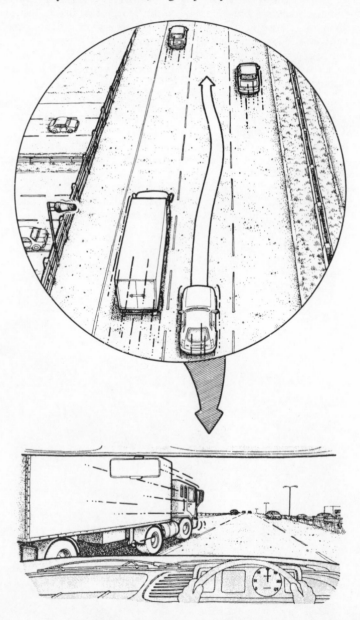

Driving through water

If you have to drive through a flood or ford, look ahead and try to judge the depth of the water. There may be a gauge which will tell you how deep it is.

Check what is happening behind you and slow down. Select first or second gear and, with a slipping clutch, keep the engine revs up. Look for any camber in the road and try to drive through very slowly at the shallowest point.

As you leave the water, try your brakes. You may need to dry them out. Drive very slowly for a few yards, pressing the brake very gently with your left foot.

How to avoid aquaplaning

If aquaplaning occurs you will have no control over the speed or direction of your vehicle.

Make sure your tyres are in good condition. With new tyres aquaplaning can occur at less than 60 mph. With worn tyres it will happen at much lower speeds.

Drive more slowly on wet surfaces. A cushion of undisplaced water can build up just ahead of the tyres. At higher speeds they can ride up onto the cushion and lose contact with the road surface.

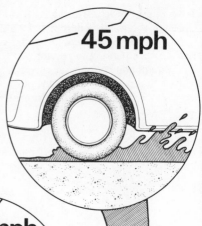

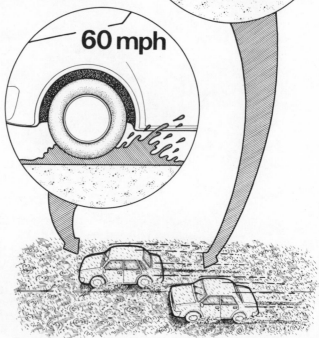

If you:

- are a conscientious driver;
- keep your car properly maintained;
- always plan well ahead;
- take into account the traffic, road and weather conditions;

you should not have to use the emergency techniques described in this section.

However, I do hope that, if the need does arise, you will be able to put the correct procedures into practice to keep yourself, your passengers, your vehicle and other road users around you safe.

5 | Good Driving Practices

This section deals with the correct procedures you should follow for driving along and dealing safely with different types of junctions.

The system of car control

There is a basic routine procedure which you should apply on the approach to all hazards. This is called 'the system of car control'.

This system is broken down into three sections:

- Mirror – Signal – Manoeuvre (M S M);
- Position – Speed – Look (P S L);
- Look – Assess – Decide – Act (L A D A).

When you see a hazard or want to change speed or direction you should:

M S M:

- Look all around and check the mirrors to find out what is happening and whether it will be safe to carry out your intended actions;
- decide whether or not any other road user (including pedestrians) will benefit from a signal. If you are turning from one road into another where your view is restricted, you should normally signal;
- carry out the manoeuvre safely by:

P S L:

- getting into the correct position;
- adjusting your speed and selecting an appropriate gear to give you maximum control; then
- look all around:

L A D A:

- look for pedestrians, obstructions or other vehicles; and
- assess whether or not it will be safe to proceed. If safe:
- make your decision and act by either:
- carrying out the manoeuvre efficiently and safely, or holding back to reassess the situation.

The system of car control

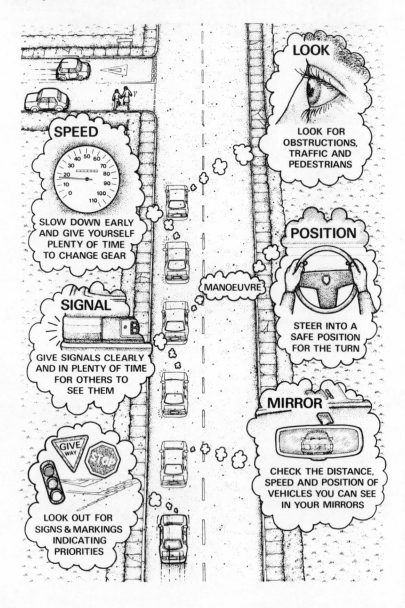

Avoid accidents caused by positioning

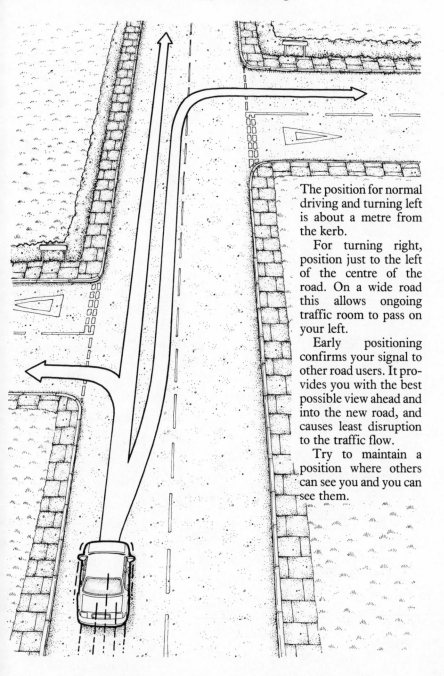

The position for normal driving and turning left is about a metre from the kerb.

For turning right, position just to the left of the centre of the road. On a wide road this allows ongoing traffic room to pass on your left.

Early positioning confirms your signal to other road users. It provides you with the best possible view ahead and into the new road, and causes least disruption to the traffic flow.

Try to maintain a position where others can see you and you can see them.

Maintaining a safe position for turning left

When you have sig-
nalled your intention
to turn left, make
sure you maintain
the correct position
about a metre from
the kerb.

This will ensure
that your back
wheels do not go
over the kerb.

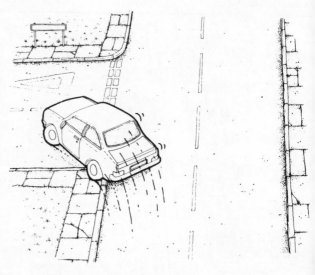

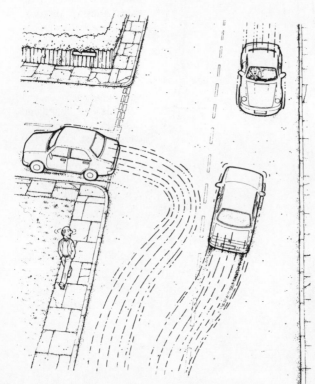

Make sure you
have slowed down
enough and selected
a gear which is
appropriate for the
corner.

This will elimi-
nate the temptation
to swing out prior to
it, putting other road
users at risk.

Give way to pedestrians crossing the road into which you are turning

Look for any pedestrians who are either about to step out or are already crossing the new road. Watch particularly for those walking with their backs to you. In some instances it may be appropriate to sound the horn lightly.

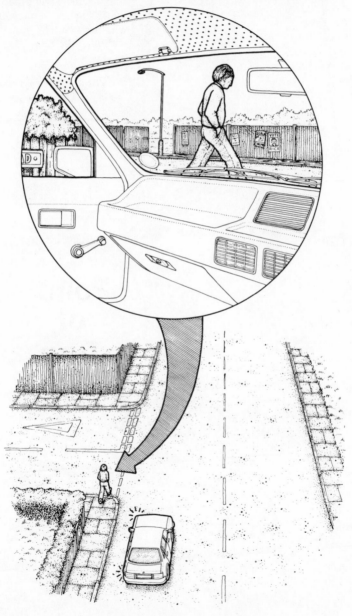

Meet oncoming traffic safely

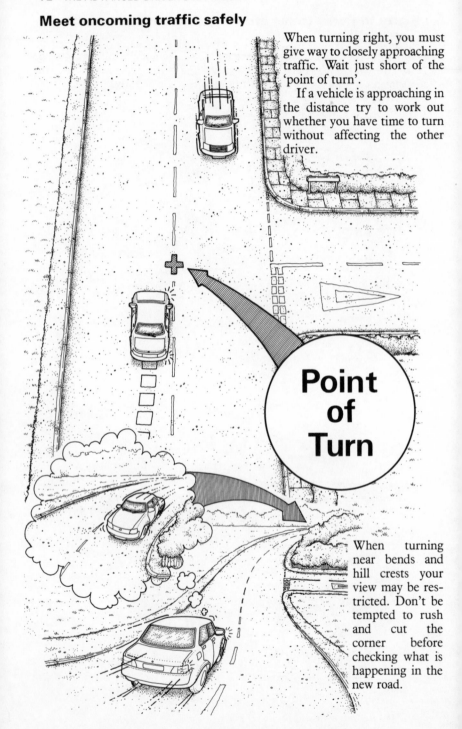

When turning right, you must give way to closely approaching traffic. Wait just short of the 'point of turn'.

If a vehicle is approaching in the distance try to work out whether you have time to turn without affecting the other driver.

Point of Turn

When turning near bends and hill crests your view may be restricted. Don't be tempted to rush and cut the corner before checking what is happening in the new road.

Look into the side road before turning

Remember you need time to check what's happening in the new road before turning. If there is an element of rush, there is an element of risk – wait!

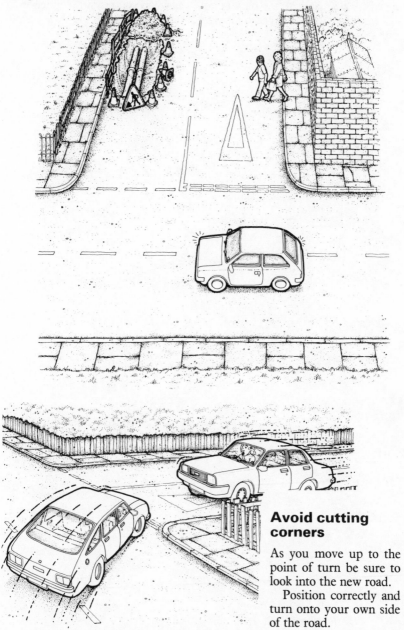

Avoid cutting corners

As you move up to the point of turn be sure to look into the new road.

Position correctly and turn onto your own side of the road.

Approaching 'T' junctions

Look out for pedestrians and hold back if they are already crossing at the junction. Approach busy shopping streets very slowly – remember, pedestrians may be walking round the back of your car when you reach the junction.

Check for signs and road markings. If there is a 'Stop' sign, make sure you do stop.

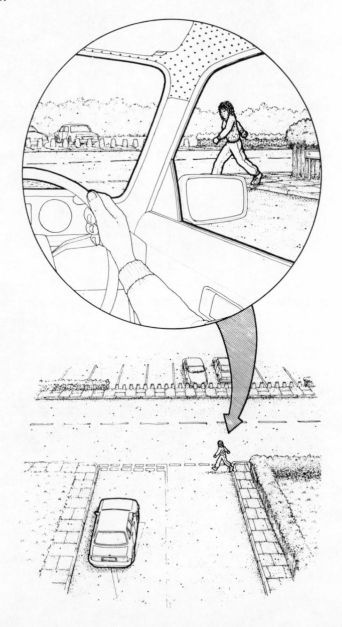

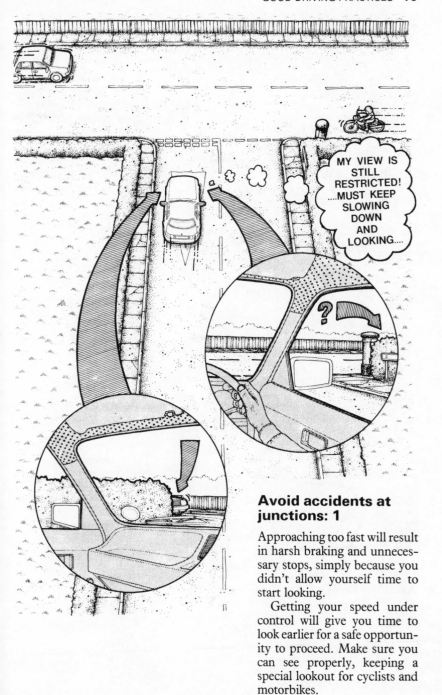

Avoid accidents at junctions: 1

Approaching too fast will result in harsh braking and unnecessary stops, simply because you didn't allow yourself time to start looking.

Getting your speed under control will give you time to look earlier for a safe opportunity to proceed. Make sure you can see properly, keeping a special lookout for cyclists and motorbikes.

Avoid accidents at junctions: 2

Vehicles parked near junctions will seriously restrict your view of traffic on the main road.

'Creep and peep' – move slowly forwards looking both ways for approaching vehicles hidden behind the obstructions.

Make sure you can see properly in both directions before deciding to proceed. Watch for vehicles approaching from your left.

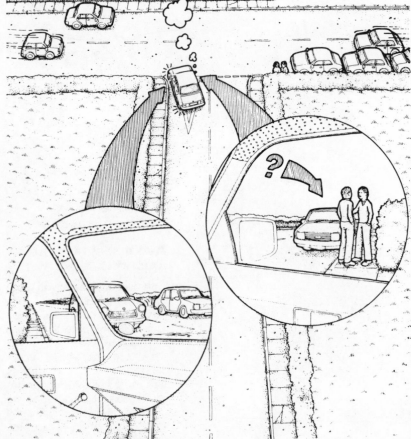

Leave drivers of large vehicles room to manoeuvre

Hold back and allow plenty of space when you see a large vehicle turning into your road. Expect them to cut the corner if they are turning right, or swing wide on it when turning left.

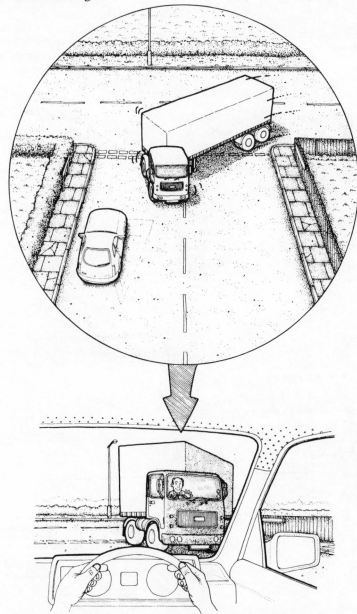

Avoiding accidents at minor crossroads

In quieter areas there are sometimes crossroads with no signs or markings indicating priorities.

These junctions can sometimes be difficult to spot. Be on the lookout for them.

Approach slowly and be prepared to give way to traffic moving along the other road. Other drivers may not be aware of the danger or may even think they have priority.

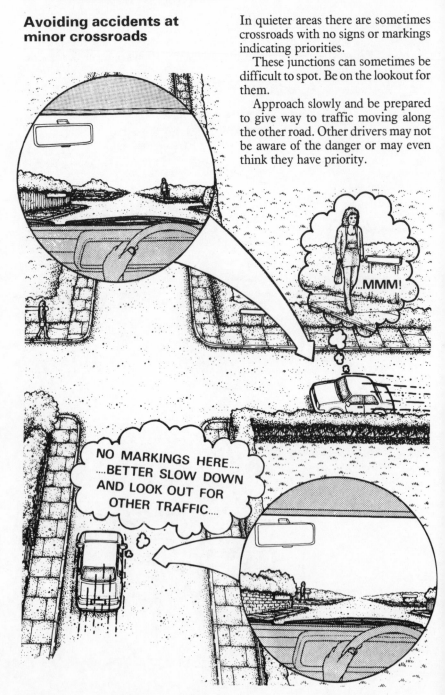

Consideration and eye contact

If you are waiting in a queue of traffic, do not block any junctions or major entrances. This will allow other vehicles to turn right into or out of the side road.

Next time you're waiting to emerge from a side road when traffic in the main road is queueing or moving slowly, look at the other drivers and make eye contact. If you can attract their attention by smiling, they are almost certain to hold back and let you out.

Approaching pedestrian crossings safely

Look well ahead for people near or within reaching distance of zebra crossings. You *must* give precedence to anyone with a foot on the crossing. Consider the possibility of them stepping out and be ready to slow down.

If you hold back early enough, pedestrians will see that you intend to stop. Try to make eye contact to help reassure them they've been seen. Allow extra time for old or disabled people, and those with prams or in charge of small children. Be cautious with children and teenagers! Some may dash straight onto the crossing at the last moment whilst others deliberately saunter across to make you wait. Be patient and move off only when it is safe.

If your view of the pavement to either side is blocked slow down. Expect someone to be crossing. Do not proceed until you can see that it is safe.

When you are parking always keep well away from any kind of pedestrian crossing!

Dealing with major crossroads

When driving straight ahead at a busy junction you should normally approach in the left lane. This eliminates the risk of other vehicles passing on your left. It also avoids unnecessary lane changes when you reach the other side of the junction, if returning to your normal driving position.

Where there are two or more lanes marked for going straight on, plan well ahead and choose the most convenient one. To do this look ahead for obstructions and use your knowledge of the area, particularly if you will be turning to the right shortly.

To turn right from a busy multi-laned road, you should normally approach in the right-hand lane. Try to maintain your speed while you check your mirrors for traffic coming up behind and at your sides and get into the correct lane early without disrupting the traffic flow. You may have to increase your speed slightly to do this. Reducing your speed in these circumstances may encourage any following drivers to overtake and prevent you from changing lanes.

Think ahead and try not to get boxed in! *Do not* change lanes suddenly!

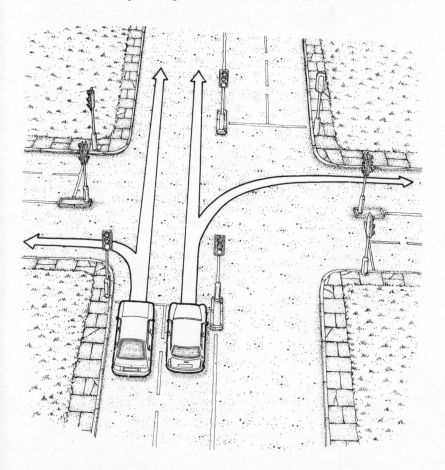

Choosing the most appropriate lane: 1

Avoid straddling lanes, particularly when approaching junctions or passing stationary vehicles. If you are in the leading vehicle and you see parked vehicles or other obstructions at the far side of a junction, approach in the right-hand lane.

However, if you are not the first in line, it may be more sensible to take the left lane. Vehicles ahead of you could be turning right. These may have to wait for oncoming traffic and you will be delayed.

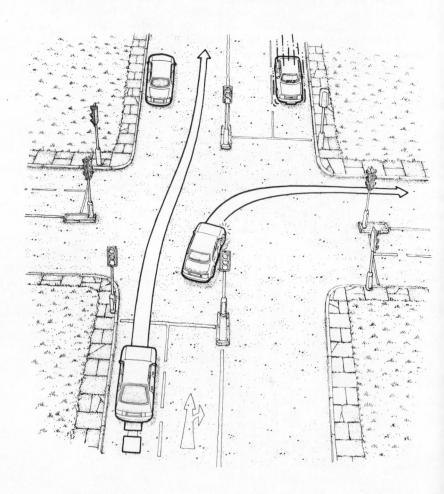

Choosing the most appropriate lane: 2

At some junctions the road markings and rules for positioning may vary. Read the road ahead and get into position as early as you can. After selecting your lane, stay in it throughout the turn.

At junctions with two or more lanes marked for one direction, choose the most convenient one. If you are turning to the right where both lanes are marked for that direction, taking the left lane will mean that you are in the correct position for normal driving afterwards.

If you are taking a subsequent road to the right, it may be more convenient to take the right-hand lane on the approach to the first junction.

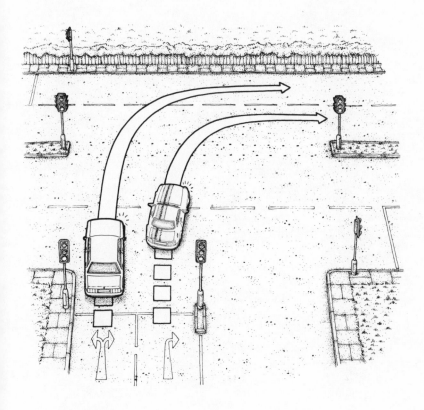

Giving way to oncoming traffic

The right turn at traffic lights is one of the most dangerous driving manoeuvres.

Even if you have a green light, be ready to give way to oncoming vehicles. Proceed over the stop line and wait just short of the point of turn for a suitable break in the traffic. If it is very busy, you may have to wait until the lights change. You must still make sure that the oncoming traffic is stopping before you turn. If you can't see what's happening in the far lane because of traffic waiting to turn, you must wait. You cannot make a safe decision to proceed until you can see properly!

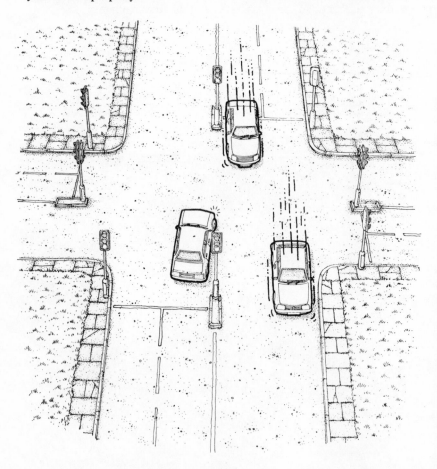

If there is a filter arrow for turning right, you may turn that way regardless of any other lights showing. However, you should still check that any oncoming vehicles are stopping before you proceed!

If there is a suitable gap in the traffic before the filter arrow appears, you may proceed as long as the main green light is still on.

Turning right at busy junctions

There are two ways in which you can turn right at busy junctions. The method you choose will normally depend on:

- the size and layout of the junction;
- any road markings telling you where to position;
- the position of any oncoming, right-turning traffic.

Turning offside to offside

If you are the first in the queue, move slowly forwards to the point of turn and, if it is safe, drive around the rear of the other vehicle. *Look and be prepared to wait for any oncoming vehicles* travelling through the junction in the far lane. If you can't see – *wait!!*

If you are the second in the queue hold back, otherwise you may prevent oncoming traffic from turning, unless the junction is large enough for two vehicles to wait in.

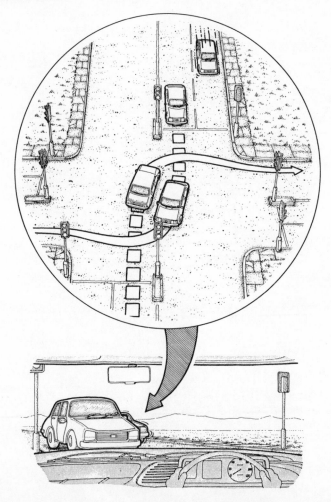

Turning nearside to nearside

Due to the size or position of other vehicles, and the junction layout or markings, this method of turning right may be appropriate. It enables more vehicles to turn in less time.

Check on the position of the oncoming vehicles. Move slowly forwards steering slightly to the right without encroaching on the oncoming traffic's lane. *Look and be prepared to wait for oncoming traffic.* If you can't see – *wait!!*

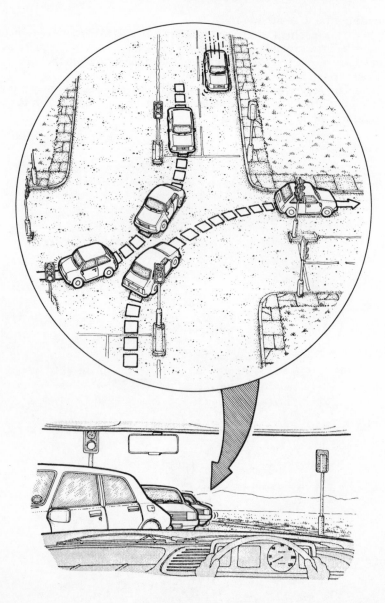

Keeping the road clear at box junctions

This type of junction has been designed to keep the traffic moving in all directions.

Even if you have a green traffic light, you should not enter the box unless your exit road is clear.

When turning right and you are waiting for oncoming traffic, you may enter the box as long as your exit road is clear.

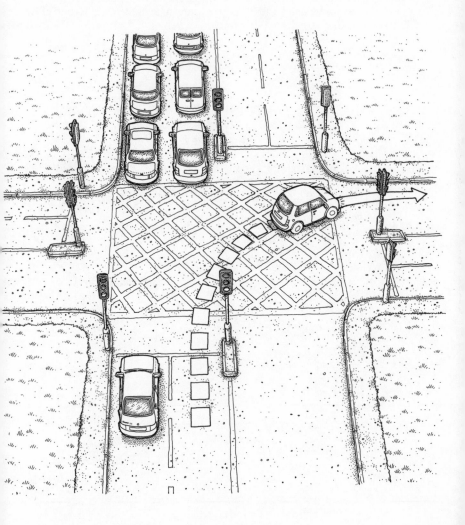

Dealing with other traffic at mini roundabouts

Mini roundabouts are becoming more common as the volume of traffic increases. They are often built into busy 'T' junctions to relieve congestion and long delays.

Drivers who have been on the road for many years often do not keep up with the changes in traffic rules and regulations. They sometimes become confused at junctions with different types of traffic control.

The general rule is similar to that at larger roundabouts: that is, you should normally give way to traffic from the right. Be on the lookout for those who appear not to understand these rules – they may pull out in front of you. Alternatively, they may be waiting for you – even though you are in the road to their left.

Dealing efficiently with roundabouts

On the approach to a roundabout look for the signs and lane markings. Make a mental note of the position of your exit road. Keep looking in both directions as you approach and give way to any traffic coming from your immediate right. Try, if it is not too busy, to time your arrival to coincide with a gap in the traffic. Keep checking to the left as well as the right – make sure the vehicle ahead of you has actually moved away before you proceed.

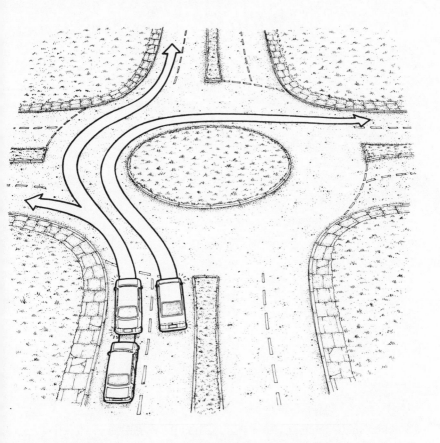

When turning left, signal and approach in the left lane. Keep the signal on and maintain the left lane on the roundabout and into the exit road.

When following the road ahead, you should normally approach in the left lane and stay in the centre of it. As you pass the exit just before yours, give a left signal for leaving the roundabout.

When turning right, signal and approach in the right-hand lane. Keep the signal on and stay in your lane as you drive round the roundabout. As you pass the exit before yours, check for vehicles in the nearside lane and change the signal to left. You should normally leave in the left lane if it is clear.

Avoiding accidents at roundabouts

Look well ahead for road markings giving directions which may vary from the basic rules. Get into position early and stay in the centre of your lane.

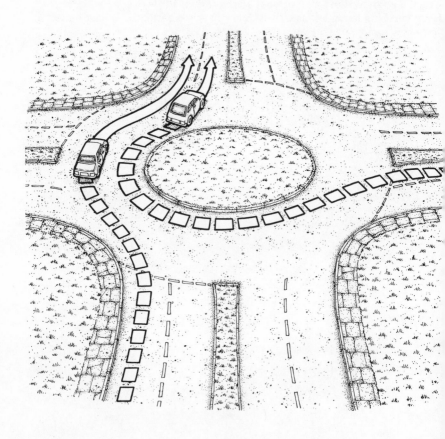

Build up and maintain a reasonable speed in the roundabout. Crawling round may result in other drivers passing on your nearside as you are trying to leave. Check for vehicles passing on your left before leaving a roundabout. Be prepared to leave the roundabout in the right-hand lane if there is traffic coming through on your left, or if the left exit lane is blocked.

Choosing the most appropriate lane for subsequent junctions

To avoid any last minute lane changes plan well ahead. If the next junction is fairly close use your local knowledge, or read any signs, and try to work out which lane you will need. For example, the lane you will need at the second of these two roundabouts should influence your choice as you approach the first.

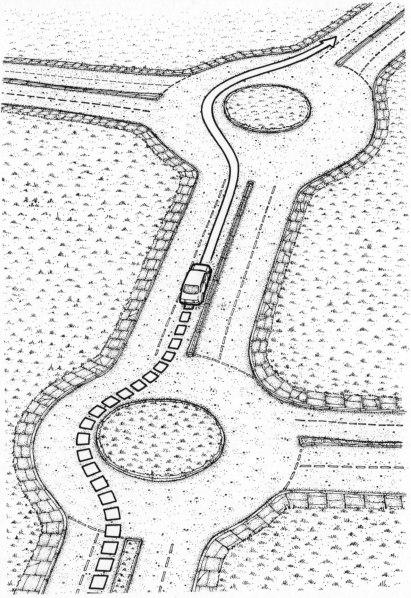

Driving in queues of slow-moving traffic

Because you may be unfamiliar with an area, you may sometimes find that you are in the wrong lane! If you are unable to change lanes safely, be prepared to miss your turning. In a queue of very slow-moving traffic it may be possible to change lanes safely by using a combination of signals, eye contact and a gradual change in position. Put your signal on and then look at the driver to your immediate rear. If you can make eye contact and smile, you are almost certain to be allowed to move over. Avoid any sudden changes in direction or spurts of speed and watch out for motorcyclists and cyclists riding between the lanes.

6 Defensive Driving Techniques

What is defensive driving?

Defensive driving involves:

- planning well ahead;
- putting into practice an efficient system of car control;
- predicting the actions of other road users;
- anticipating possible as well as actual problems; and
- compensating for the mistakes of others.

This section will help you recognise hazards earlier and avoid problems so that your driving becomes more enjoyable.

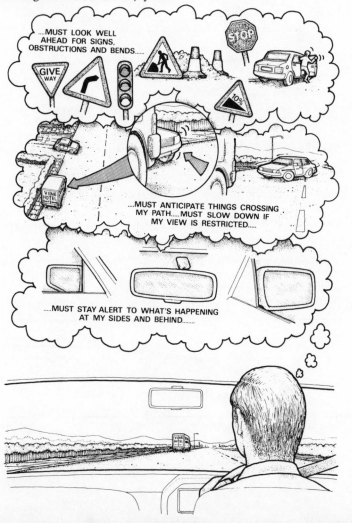

Avoiding accidents when manoeuvring

Before reversing out of a driveway, look for pedestrians on the pavement. Move back very slowly and keep checking for them. If your vision is restricted by hedges or fencing, use your horn as a warning.

Before carrying out any reversing manoeuvre, check to the front, rear and sides for other road users and obstructions. Turn well round in your seat until you can see clearly where you are going. Keep a special lookout for pedestrians and move slowly, particularly if people are standing nearby or if your view is at all restricted. Keep looking all around for approaching traffic as you manoeuvre. Remember, the other driver has priority. If anyone approaches, wait and let them make the decision to proceed or wait.

Avoid reversing from side roads into main roads, or turning round on busy roads where you may cause inconvenience or danger to others.

Checking blind areas before moving off and opening doors

Before you drive away, take an initial look to the front and in the mirrors as you get ready to move. To be one hundred per cent sure that it's safe to move out, check the blind area and be prepared to wait.

If you are parking on the road, check to the side before opening your door.

Can you always stop within the distance you can see to be clear?

You should maintain margins for error and drive at speeds so that you can always stop comfortably well within the distance you can see is clear.

Take nothing for granted and expect things to change!

Look for people and other vehicles and predict the potential for their movement into or across your path. Be ready to slow down!

Stationary vehicles, particularly buses, restrict your view of people crossing the road. Remember they may not be able to see you either!

Pedestrians very often get off the bus, walk round its front or rear, and step straight out into the road.

Be prepared to slow down and allow extra clearance. As you approach, look through windows and underneath the vehicles for signs of movement or other danger.

Forward planning skills

If you are approaching a red traffic light, be prepared to slow down early. This will give more time for the lights to change and means that you will either be able to proceed efficiently if they do, or stop comfortably if they don't.

Remember that all colours except green mean stop. When you are approaching a green light, try to predict when it may change and be ready to pull up. At some point on the approach, however, you will find yourself too close to stop safely. Once past this point you should normally continue if it is safe.

Keep assessing the situation as you approach. Check how close the following vehicle is and how fast it is travelling. Continually reassess what you will do if the lights change as this will save critical seconds. It means you will be able to make an instant decision to go on or stop if the amber light comes on.

Remember that not everyone 'drives by the book'. When you approach any green light, look and be prepared to hold back for vehicles proceeding through the junction on the wrong colour, oncoming drivers turning across your path, or pedestrians crossing the road.

Being aware of what is happening behind you

As well as planning well ahead, it is equally important to keep in constant touch with what is happening to the sides and rear of your vehicle.

Make sure your mirrors are adjusted to give you maximum-view all-round vision with the minimum of head movement. Extra blind-spot mirrors can be particularly useful if you do a lot of driving on dual carriageways and motorways.

Check your mirrors frequently as you drive along. With experience your peripheral vision subconsciously detects movement in the mirrors and should attract your attention at critical times.

Making regular mirror checks will enable you to judge the speed and distance of any following traffic more precisely. It will also help ensure that you are aware when a vehicle has moved into the blind areas at your sides.

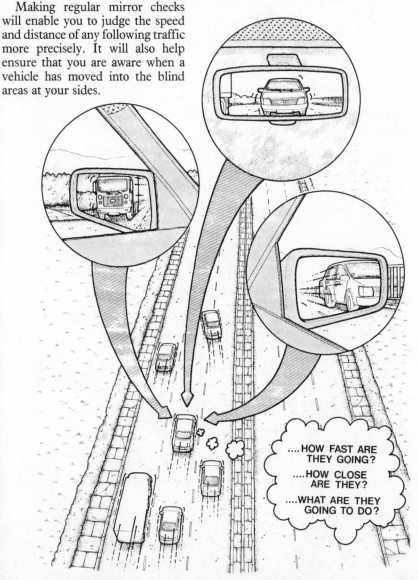

....HOW FAST ARE THEY GOING?

....HOW CLOSE ARE THEY?

....WHAT ARE THEY GOING TO DO?

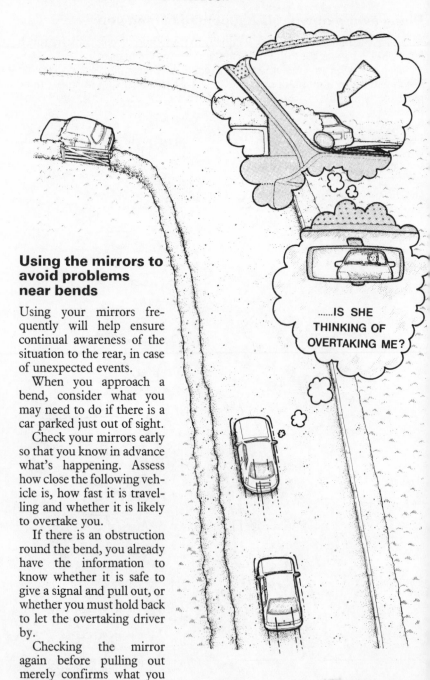

Using the mirrors to avoid problems near bends

Using your mirrors frequently will help ensure continual awareness of the situation to the rear, in case of unexpected events.

When you approach a bend, consider what you may need to do if there is a car parked just out of sight.

Check your mirrors early so that you know in advance what's happening. Assess how close the following vehicle is, how fast it is travelling and whether it is likely to overtake you.

If there is an obstruction round the bend, you already have the information to know whether it is safe to give a signal and pull out, or whether you must hold back to let the overtaking driver by.

Checking the mirror again before pulling out merely confirms what you already know.

Avoiding accidents with vehicles overtaking you

As you drive along be aware of any vehicles about to overtake, do not accelerate as they pass, and leave them plenty of room to get back in.

Use your side mirrors before turning, changing lanes and leaving roundabouts.

Before indicating to turn right, check your mirrors to ensure you are not being over-taken. If anyone is approaching at speed, be prepared for them to pass.

After indicating to make a turn, make sure any following driver has seen and is respond-ing to your signal. Decide whether or not your intended actions can be carried out safely. When safe, confirm your signal by taking up the correct position in the road.

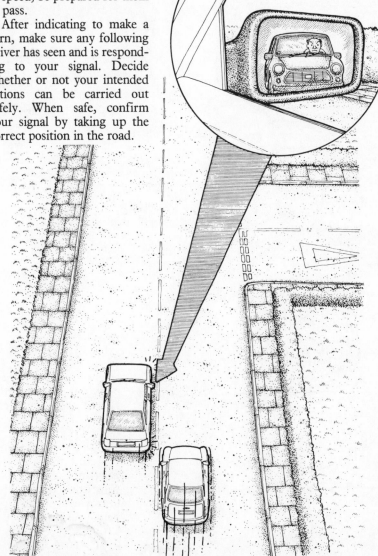

Using the mirrors to avoid accidents with cyclists and motorcyclists

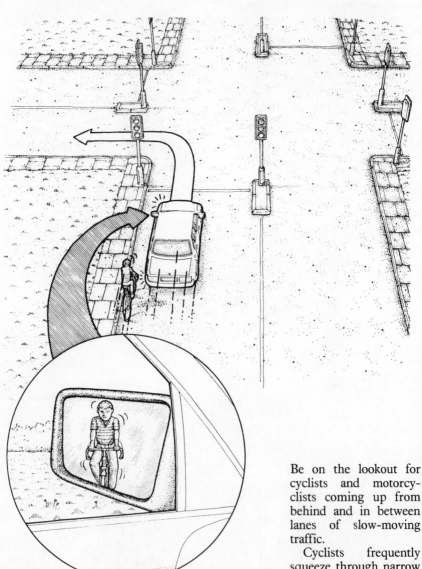

Be on the lookout for cyclists and motorcyclists coming up from behind and in between lanes of slow-moving traffic.

Cyclists frequently squeeze through narrow gaps in traffic queues. Check the nearside door mirror and blind spot before moving off to turn left.

Check for pedestrians before turning right

If you have to wait for a change in the lights before the oncoming traffic stops, remember to look into the new road while you are waiting. There may be pedestrians crossing the road, particularly if there is a pelican crossing incorporated into the traffic lights.

If their light is on green, proceed through the junction and then wait at the crossing until you can clear it safely.

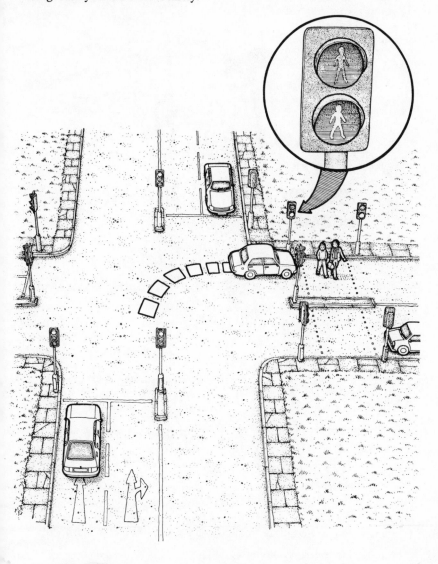

Do you always need to signal?

Signals should be used if they will help to warn or inform any other road user of your intentions. If you are unsure whether a signal is needed, it is usually safer to give one. However, giving a signal at the wrong time *will not make an unsafe action safe.*

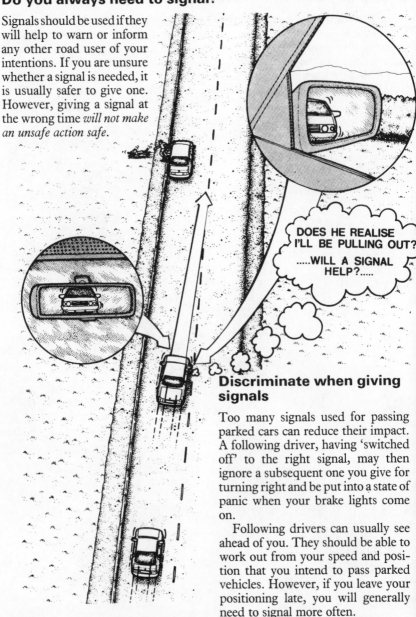

DOES HE REALISE I'LL BE PULLING OUT?

.....WILL A SIGNAL HELP?.....

Discriminate when giving signals

Too many signals used for passing parked cars can reduce their impact. A following driver, having 'switched off' to the right signal, may then ignore a subsequent one you give for turning right and be put into a state of panic when your brake lights come on.

Following drivers can usually see ahead of you. They should be able to work out from your speed and position that you intend to pass parked vehicles. However, if you leave your positioning late, you will generally need to signal more often.

Signals are required more frequently for passing obstructions when:

- following traffic is coming up fast; or
- is already in a lane to your right; or
- you are driving in fog or poor light conditions; or
- they are round a bend or in a hollow.

Timing signals correctly to avoid confusion

Signals in some circumstances need to be delayed, for example if you want to turn left but have to move out for parked vehicles on the approach to the junction.

Signals given at the wrong time may panic others into taking unnecessary evasive action. Before giving any signal you should consider its effect on them.

If you are taking a second turning on the left, wait until you are up to the first road before signalling for the second.

This will avoid the driver in the first road pulling out in front of you because he thinks you are turning in.

However, if someone is following closely you should try to give as much warning as is safely possible.

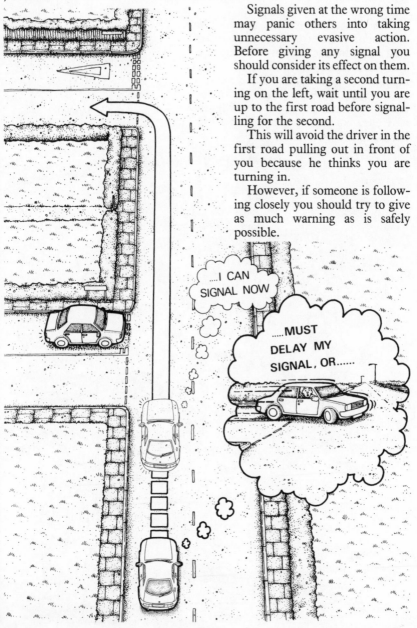

Give way to oncoming traffic

Where there are obstructions on your side, remember it is the oncoming driver's priority. Be prepared to hold back and give way. Position towards the centre of the road. This will give you a better view of the road ahead and reduce the risk of becoming boxed in.

Ideally, when you pass a parked vehicle, you should try to give it three to four feet clearance. However, in busy conditions, it may be necessary to keep the traffic moving and you may have to leave a much smaller gap. By slowing right down and feeling your way through, you will still have plenty of time to react should a door open or other problem arise.

Dealing safely with oncoming vehicles

To assume that oncoming drivers will give way to you because there are obstructions on their side of the road may result in serious problems.

No matter whose priority it may be, you should be prepared to give way.

Look ahead and work out how long it will take the other driver to reach the obstruction. Even if you only suspect they are not going to wait, hold back and allow them time to get through safely.

As long as you make the 'hold back' decision early enough, minor adjustments to your speed will normally be all that is needed.

When oncoming drivers give way to you, help to promote good manners by acknowledging the courtesy.

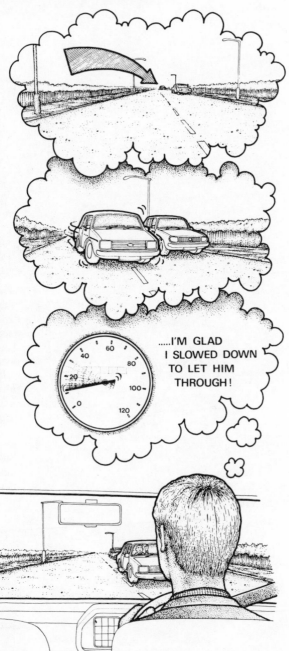

Avoiding accidents with vehicles ahead: 1

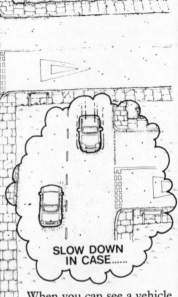

SLOW DOWN IN CASE......

WHAT IF.....

When you can see a vehicle ahead signalling to turn, you can expect it to slow down to execute the manoeuvre. Anticipate a change in its position and speed.

If it is turning right, position well over to the left so that you can pass on its nearside.

Should the driver ahead need to wait for oncoming traffic, anticipate this. Be prepared to hold back if there is not enough room to get through safely.

If the driver ahead is signalling left, the vehicle may either be stopping or turning. Check your mirrors and move into an overtaking position, but hold back. What if ... it can't turn because of pedestrians crossing the road or there are other obstructions? Don't be tempted to swing out around it, especially if there is oncoming traffic.

Avoiding accidents with vehicles ahead: 2

When driving at higher speeds, look and plan even further ahead. Watch out for obstructions in your lane, for vehicles slowing down prior to turning, or anyone waiting in the central reserve.

Avoiding accidents with buses

What if . . . the bus driver suddenly pulls up with little or no warning? Keep well back. Watch out for signs that they may be stopping. For example,

- look for brake lights which may come on before the indicator;
- look to see what's happening on the bus – if pedestrians are getting up there is probably a bus stop not far away;
- look ahead for people queueing at bus stops.

Follow in an overtaking position towards the centre of the road. This will give a better view ahead. Hold back until there is a safe opportunity to get by.

Expect bus drivers to signal and move straight out just as you are approaching or passing. Be prepared to hold back and let them go!

As you pass, leave extra clearance to provide a better view into the blind area. Be on the lookout for people stepping out from behind the bus and check all around, there may be someone about to run across the road to catch it!

Avoiding accidents with cyclists: 1

If you can't overtake a cyclist safely, stay well back and follow in a position out towards the centre of the road. This will help avoid the cyclist becoming nervous. Staying in this position will also make overtaking much easier when an opportunity arises and also prevent following drivers boxing you in. When you pass, try to give at least five to six feet clearance.

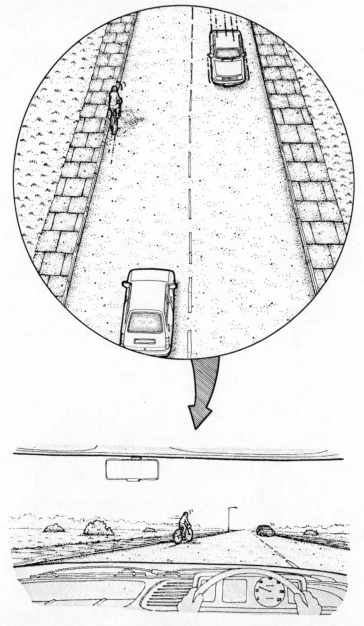

Avoiding accidents with cyclists: 2

Leave cyclists plenty of clearance. The closer you get the more they will wobble! If you are unable to pass, keep in an overtaking position but stay well back until you are sure you can get by safely.

Cyclists' steering often becomes erratic when they are struggling to pedal uphill. Expect them to swerve to avoid roadside grates and potholes.

Remember to look carefully when emerging from side roads. Cyclists usually ride along close to the kerb and are sometimes difficult to see. Think once, think twice – think *bike!*

Cyclists are also difficult to see at night and in poor weather conditions. They often ride without lights and wear dark clothing.

'Look no hands!' Watch out for this and other unusual actions such as 'wheelies'.

You would not want a child's life on your conscience! Hold back if you sense something is about to happen. Be patient and allow even more space.

Youngsters don't always read or understand Highway Code rules. They are unlikely to be aware of the importance of correct signalling and positioning.

Watch out for youngsters signalling to go one way and then turning the other.

What if . . . they are riding along on the wrong side of the road, or pull straight out of a junction without looking?

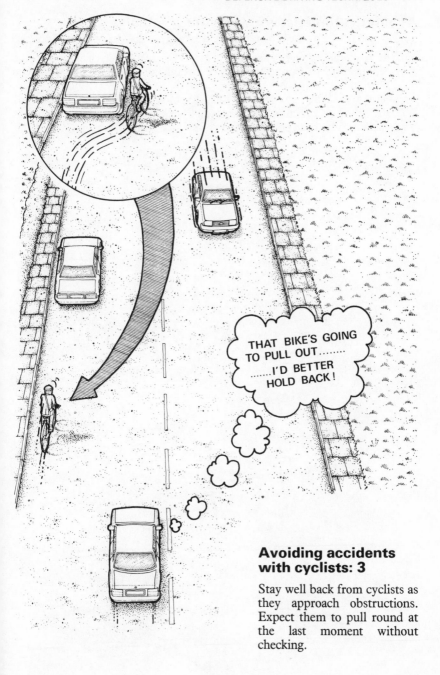

Avoiding accidents with cyclists: 3

Stay well back from cyclists as they approach obstructions. Expect them to pull round at the last moment without checking.

Avoiding problems with emerging vehicles

As you approach side roads, try to make eye contact with drivers waiting to pull out. At least then you can be sure they've seen you. Watch out for those approaching too fast, especially if they're looking the other way! What will you do if they pull out?

Junctions are often obscured by parked vehicles. Remember the emerging driver's sightlines will also be restricted. Check your mirrors and cover the brake pedal ready for action even though you have priority.

How you can avoid accidents with right turning vehicles

It is dangerous to assume that others will give way to you when they are turning right. Be prepared! What will you do if they cut across your path?

This problem often happens at traffic lights particularly, if the oncoming driver cannot see your car because you are hidden by vehicles in the lane to your right!

Be prepared to hold back if you think an oncoming driver may turn across your path.

Judge the speed, distance and time it will take them to reach the point of turn. Look at the driver, try to make eye contact and be on your guard.

Remember, as long as your decision is made early enough, minor adjustments to your speed are all that will normally be needed.

It is of little consequence whose priority it was if an accident puts you in hospital.

Approaching bends and hill crests safely

Will you be ready if there is a vehicle just out of sight? It could be turning across your path. There may be pedestrians crossing the road just round the bend. Be ready to slow down!

There could be oncoming traffic having to drive in the centre of the road, because of an obstruction.

Be ready to hold back and give them time to return to their own side of the road.

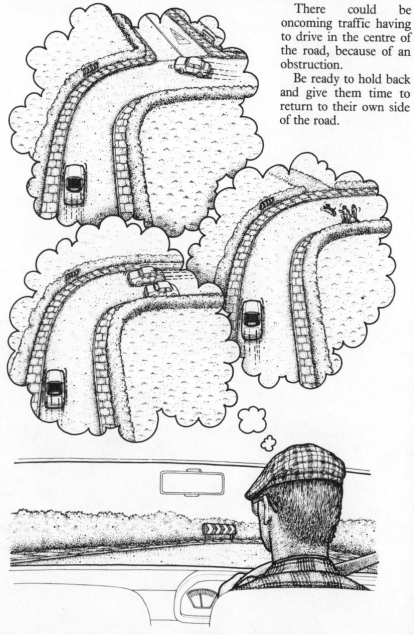

Positioning for dealing safely with bends

Approach right bends well over to the left to give a better view of the road ahead. Complete your slowing down, and any necessary gear change, so that you can drive through the bend at a constant speed.

When you are positioning for left bends you should take into consideration:

- the width of the road;
- how far you can see;
- the road markings; and, if you are preparing for an advanced driving test:
- the position preferred by the examining body.

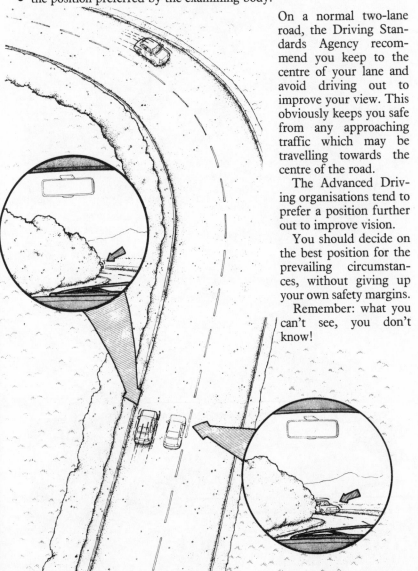

On a normal two-lane road, the Driving Standards Agency recommend you keep to the centre of your lane and avoid driving out to improve your view. This obviously keeps you safe from any approaching traffic which may be travelling towards the centre of the road.

The Advanced Driving organisations tend to prefer a position further out to improve vision.

You should decide on the best position for the prevailing circumstances, without giving up your own safety margins.

Remember: what you can't see, you don't know!

Make sure others can see you!

Using the correct lights not only helps you see more clearly, it will also help ensure that others can see you!

At night and in poor daylight conditions such as fog, heavy rain and falling snow, use your dipped headlights.

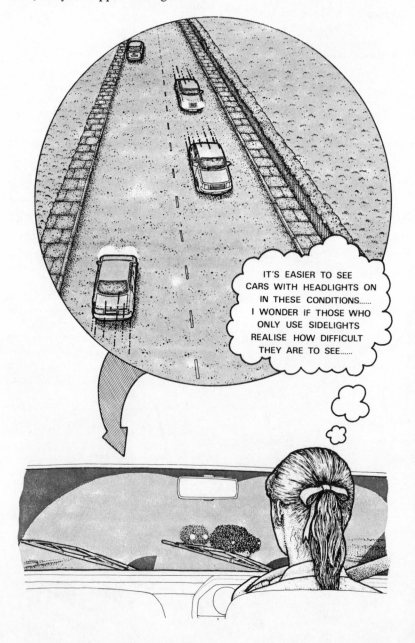

Avoiding accidents when you drive in the dark

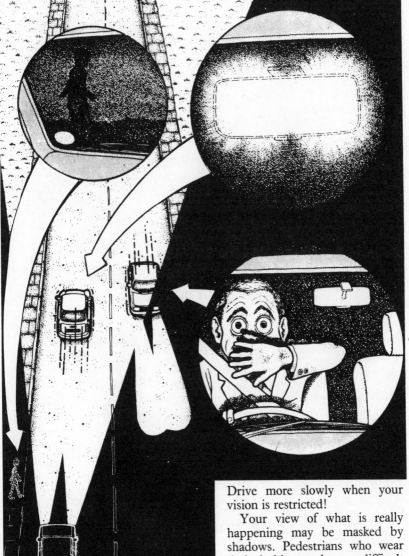

Drive more slowly when your vision is restricted!

Your view of what is really happening may be masked by shadows. Pedestrians who wear dark clothing can be very difficult to see and cyclists sometimes ride without lights.

Dip your headlights so that you don't dazzle oncoming drivers. Remember also to dip them when you are following others.

How to avoid accidents when driving in fog

As a good driver you should avoid parking on the road in fog! If you have no choice, it will be safer to leave your sidelights on.

Keep your windows free of condensation and use your wipers. Drive slowly, stay well back from the vehicle ahead and watch out for obstructions in the road.

Other drivers may not have their headlights on so use your ears as well as your eyes. Wind your window down and listen for other traffic before moving out of junctions.

When waiting to turn right from a main road, keep your foot on the brake pedal so the brake lights give extra warning of your presence.

Avoiding accidents at pedestrian crossings

Do not overtake on the approach to a crossing. If you are driving in lanes you may pull up level with the leading vehicle but do not pass it. Where there is a refuge in the centre, look for pedestrians on the other half of the crossing who may be nearing it. Although you should normally treat this as two separate crossings, the pedestrians may not have read the Highway Code and could walk straight through onto your half.

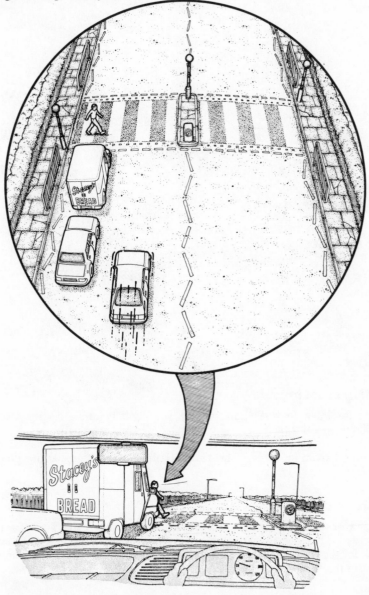

Avoiding accidents at pelican crossings

Approach with caution. If there are people standing nearby, the lights could change at any moment. Even if there is no one around the lights could change.

Give precedence to people on the crossing when the amber light is flashing. Once they have crossed you may proceed but watch out for people dashing out on the wrong colour and be prepared to let them go.

Puffin crossings

These are similar to the Pelican crossing except that an infra-red scanner holds the lights on red if there are still pedestrians on the crossing.

If there are no pedestrians in the range of the scanner, the signals should remain on green for traffic. There is no flashing amber signal at this type of crossing.

Toucan crossings

These are crossings for cyclists and pedestrians, hence the name Toucan – 'two can cross'. They can cross at the same time, cyclists being allowed to ride over. Look for the traffic signals and zig-zag markings. There is no flashing amber phase at this type of crossing.

How to avoid accidents near parked vehicles

Drive more slowly, looking for signs of movement through windows and for feet between the obstructions. What if . . . ! Other drivers may move out of side roads because their sightlines are also restricted by the obstructions.

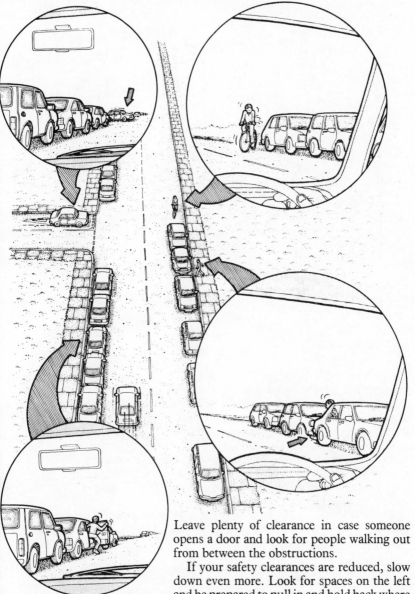

Leave plenty of clearance in case someone opens a door and look for people walking out from between the obstructions.

If your safety clearances are reduced, slow down even more. Look for spaces on the left and be prepared to pull in and hold back where necessary for oncoming vehicles.

Avoiding accidents with pedestrians: 1

Two out of every three pedestrians killed or seriously injured are either under 15 or over 60. People in these age groups may not be able to judge your speed and distance. Will you be ready if they step out into the road?

Be patient with older people – they may be slow and hesitant. Show consideration for the disabled and look out for people with white sticks or guide dogs. Those who have hearing difficulties may not hear your vehicle approaching.

Slow down in busy pedestrian areas and expect shoppers to step out into the road. On housing estates watch out for people stepping out from behind mobile shops. Check your mirror and be ready to stop if necessary.

If you have to drive over a pavement to enter a property, you must 'give way' to pedestrians. When driving onto the pavement from a blind exit, move slowly and be prepared to tap your horn lightly.

Drive with consideration for others. A cold, dirty shower is not very pleasant – in wet weather avoid driving through puddles. If you can't avoid them – slow down!

Avoiding accidents with pedestrians: 2

Where pedestrians are walking or standing close to the kerb check your mirrors. Slow down and be prepared to move further out as you approach. Even a slight adjustment in your position and speed will give you more time and clearance should anyone step out.

Drive slowly near schools, particularly at the times when children come and go. Be extra careful near ice cream vans, particularly if there are unrestrained children around.

The young are quick and impulsive. They are usually too busy playing to notice you and they can move unexpectedly. Be prepared to stop! As you approach them, check on following traffic and slow down to a speed at which you can pull up if a child runs out.

Avoiding accidents with pedestrians: 3

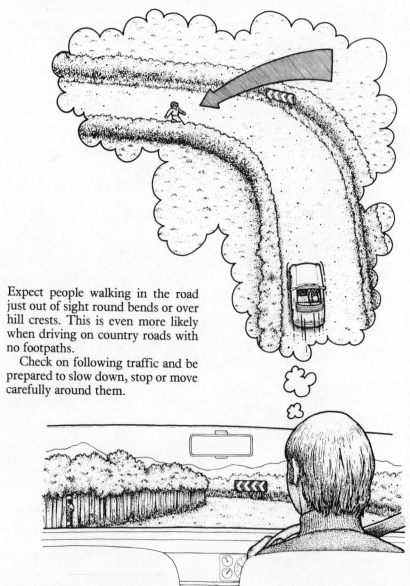

Expect people walking in the road just out of sight round bends or over hill crests. This is even more likely when driving on country roads with no footpaths.

Check on following traffic and be prepared to slow down, stop or move carefully around them.

Joggers seem to insist on running in the road! Watch out for them, particularly at night when they can be very difficult to see. They may be even more obscure if they are wearing dark tracksuits, even on well lit roads!

In icy weather pedestrians frequently walk in the road to avoid slipping on pavements. Be patient and make allowances for them.

Avoiding accidents with animals

When you see any loose animals, assess the risk, check on following traffic and be prepared to slow down. What will you do if one runs into the road? If this happens, check your mirrors and, if safe, keep both hands on the wheel to maintain a straight course and brake firmly.

Hold well back from horses until you can leave enough room to pass safely. Drive past under quiet, gentle acceleration and don't use the horn!

Avoiding accidents on country roads

Don't be lulled into a false sense of security because you are away from the bustle of town traffic. The countryside holds its own special dangers. Drive slowly on narrow roads and be prepared to stop opposite or pull in to passing places. Keep your speed down through villages and near farm entrances. Remember – where you can't see round the bend, you don't know what's there!

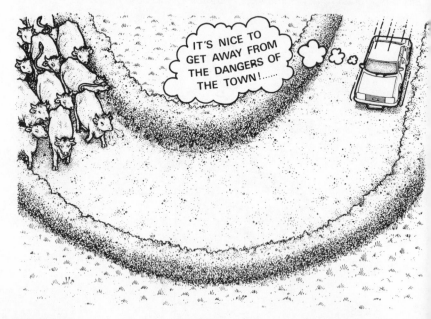

Drive slowly on muddy roads and where your view is restricted. Expect to find obstructions such as slow-moving agricultural vehicles. Be patient if you get stuck behind one on a narrow road. When it is obviously unsafe to overtake it really isn't worth the frustration and risk involved in trying.

Take care when driving through country parks where the roads are unfenced, particularly at lambing time.

Following other vehicles safely

When travelling at speeds of over 40 mph keep at least a two-second gap between you and the vehicle ahead. One yard for each mph of your speed is normally considered to be a safe following distance.

To improve your view of the road ahead, stay further back from large and slow-moving vehicles. This position will also give you more time to respond if the driver ahead stops.

If you feel a following driver is threatening you, don't be 'pushed' into driving faster. In fact you need to drop even further back to create more braking distance so that the driver behind will also be able to pull up safely if necessary.

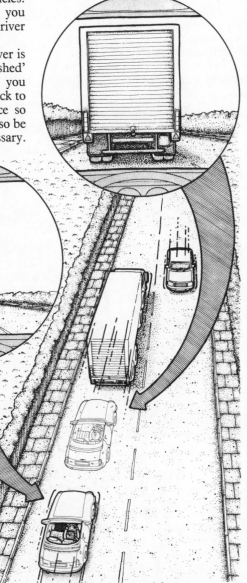

Overtaking safely

To overtake safely you need a long straight stretch of road where there are no oncoming vehicles, obstructions or side roads. To get a good view, stay well back, moving over to look along the nearside of the vehicle you are about to overtake. Then, move over until you can see along the offside.

A lower gear will give you more sustained power to get by efficiently. Check all around to see whether it is still safe and decide whether a signal will help anyone, including the driver you are about to pass.

Accelerate quickly past, leaving plenty of clearance, and pull back in to the left as soon as you can do so without cutting in.

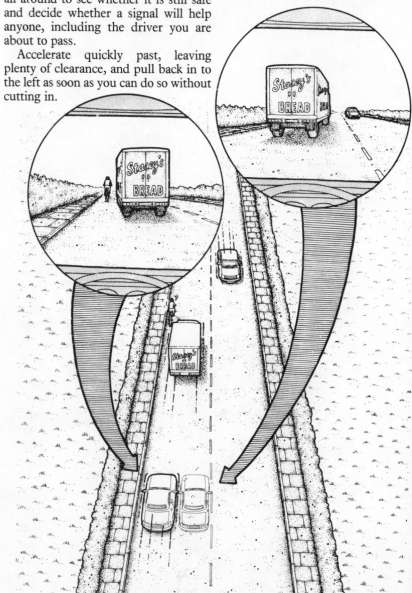

When in doubt avoid overtaking

Overtaking is one of the most dangerous manoeuvres! Decide if the benefits are worth the risks involved! Ask yourself: 'Is it safe? Is it legal? Is it necessary?'

There is little point in overtaking if you will shortly be turning or if there is a problem ahead.

What if . . . the driver ahead pulls out to pass a cyclist or parked car which you haven't noticed?

Is the other driver turning off? Is anyone overtaking you?

Places where you should not overtake

Consider how far you will be travelling on the wrong side of the road while overtaking. You should also take into consideration the distance which will be covered by any oncoming vehicle in the distance. If you are travelling at 60 mph and there is a vehicle doing the same just out of your view, this makes an approach speed of 120 mph!

Do not overtake on the approach to pedestrian crossings!

What if ... your view of approaching traffic is restricted by a bend or hill crest, or a car turns out of the side road?

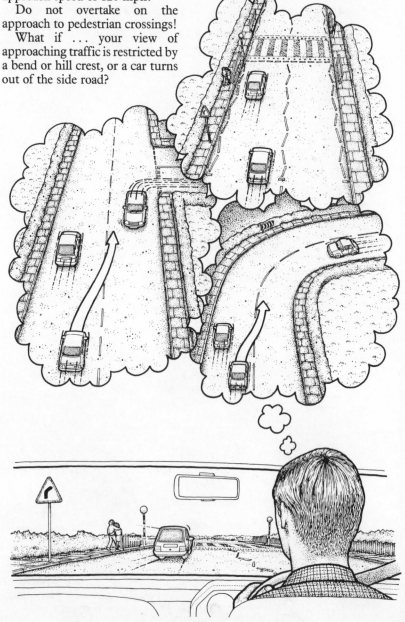

Avoiding accidents when driving in lanes

When there is more than one lane on your side of the road, you should normally keep to the left unless turning right or overtaking. Drive in the centre of your lane, look and plan well ahead, and check your mirrors regularly. This will help you to avoid becoming boxed in behind parked vehicles.

When you see others wanting to move out into the lane ahead of you, hold back for them, or if there is a third lane and you can move over safely, do so.

On one-way streets expect traffic to pass you on either side. Pedestrians are sometimes confused about which way to look for traffic. Watch out for them stepping into the road looking the other way.

Avoiding accidents with vehicles at your sides

Avoid driving in the blind spots of drivers in lanes to your sides. Stay back from the vehicle ahead so that you can be seen in the door mirrors.

Drivers of large vehicles may need extra room through some junctions. They may swing out before turning left, or position close to the left prior to turning right into an entrance or narrow road.

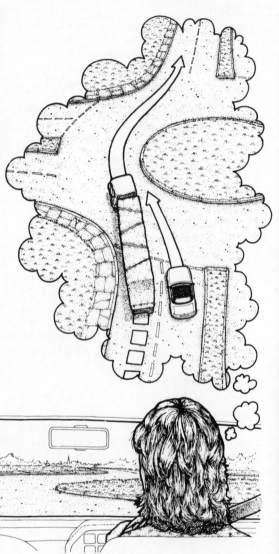

The sheer size of a vehicle may mean the driver has no option but to cut corners or take an unusual course through roundabouts.

Avoiding collisions when turning right onto dual carriageways

Look at the road layout and decide whether there will be enough room in the central reserve to protect you from traffic moving along the dual carriageway.

Avoiding motorway accidents

You should stay in the left lane under normal circumstances. Drive at least two seconds back from the vehicle ahead. If the left lane is congested with slow, heavy traffic, you may drive in the centre lane. Return to the left as soon as you can. The right-hand lane is for overtaking only.

Very often drivers stay in the centre lane when they could use the left one. This makes overtaking difficult for faster drivers approaching from the rear in the left lane. They have to move out across two lanes to overtake.

Use all of your mirrors frequently and avoid changing lanes suddenly or unnecessarily.

If you can't move over safely, adjust your speed to allow others to move into the lane ahead of you from slip roads and where motorways merge.

When leaving the motorway, get into the left lane in good time. Do not start slowing down too early as this will affect the traffic on the main carriageway.

After driving for long periods at high speed, remember, you may still be going faster than you think you are.

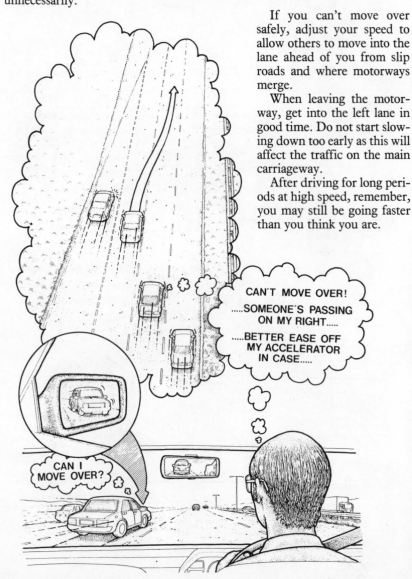

Avoiding motorway disasters

There is a national speed limit of 70 mph on most of our motorways. However, the average speed of the majority of drivers using them is much higher.

High speed alone does not necessarily kill. Driving much too close to the vehicle ahead, combined with speeds far too high for the road and traffic conditions, all too often results in multi-vehicle accidents.

Defensive driving means you should:

- drive at speeds which are appropriate for the road and traffic conditions;
- concentrate, stay alert and read the road well ahead at all times;
- keep constantly in touch with what is happening to your rear and sides;
- keep well back from the vehicle ahead – put the 'two-second' rule into practice and allow even more stopping distance in wet conditions;
- be prepared to compensate for the actions of others;
- drive more slowly in poor light and weather conditions;
- do not dazzle others or mask your own brake lights by using high intensity rear lights at the wrong times.

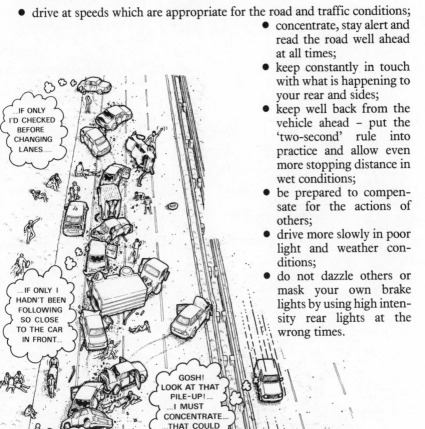

Keeping yourself safe at level crossings

There are two main types of level crossing. Most have either full or half barriers; some are ungated. Both types may be controlled by a steady amber light followed by two flashing red lights. This is a warning that a train is approaching. A warning sound will accompany the lights.

A warning sign on the approach will tell you which type of crossing you are approaching.

Gated crossings

To protect yourself and your passengers you should never:

- drive onto the crossing unless the road is clear at the other side;
- drive nose-to-tail over it;
- stop on or just after it;
- park close to it;
- move onto it after the lights come on;
- stop on the crossing if the light or warning sound comes on – keep going;
- zig-zag around the barriers;
- start moving if the red lights continue to flash or the alarm sound changes in tone – another train is approaching.

Ungated crossings

Some level crossings have neither gates nor barriers. They will normally have either flashing lights or 'Give Way' signs. Remember, if you cannot clear the crossing, do not drive onto it – a train may be approaching.

At some crossings there are barriers or gates, but no lights. Stop when the gates begin to close.

Dealing safely with trams

Trams, or Light Rapid Transport systems, are being reintroduced in some of the larger cities to encourage commuters to use public transport in order to ease congestion.

Traffic signs warn of tram crossings and you should treat them the same as you would level crossings. Look for:

- tram lanes, marked by white lines;
- a different type of road surface;
- traffic lights;
- the track crossing from one side of the road to the other;
- the road narrowing;
- pedestrians running to catch the tram.

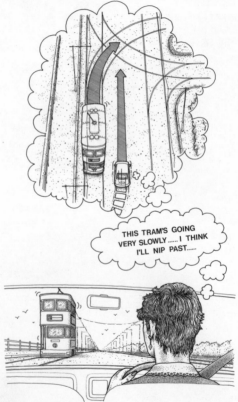

THIS TRAM'S GOING VERY SLOWLY...... I THINK I'LL NIP PAST......

Remember trams are often longer than buses, and can be up to 60 metres (196 ft) in length. They run very quietly – before you cross the tram lines look both ways and take extra care. Always give way to trams – do not try to race them.

If there is a tram stop without a platform, do not drive between the tram lines and the left-hand kerb.

Protect your car and other road users!

Park well away from bends, junctions, hill tops and any other place where the view of other drivers is already restricted. Inconsiderate parking forces drivers onto the wrong side of the road where any approaching traffic is hidden from view. Always apply the parking brake before leaving your car. As an additional precaution, when you park on steep hills select first or reverse gear and point the wheels in towards the kerb.

Using the hazard warning lights does not make parking in an illegal position legal! Try to park on straight parts of the road in safe, convenient and legal places. On narrower roads, park well away from any vehicles already parked on the opposite side. Avoid parking near schools and do not block entrances to hospitals, fire stations, doctors' surgeries and private driveways. Remember to leave the sidelights on if the road is poorly lit or if the speed limit is over 30 mph.

Looking after yourself and your property

In a changing world there are many problems being experienced by motorists. There is a need to protect yourself and your property. You can do this by:

- keeping your doors locked when driving in built-up areas;
- keeping valuables out of sight and not on the passenger seat;
- carrying a first-aid kit and fire extinguisher;
- fitting an immobiliser;
- placing a warning triangle on the road to the rear should you break down;
- parking in well lit areas.

If you are a woman travelling alone it is advisable to:

- make sure your car is well maintained to reduce the risk of breakdown;
- let someone know your route and your approximate time of arrival if you are travelling long distances or in unfamiliar places;
- keep your handbag under your seat;
- carry a hands-free mobile phone in the car;
- if you break down on a motorway stop near an emergency telephone if you can. If not, the arrows on the posts tell you which way to go to the nearest one. Make it clear you are alone and then return to your car and lock yourself in;
- do not open the window or door to anyone unless you are absolutely sure of their credentials;
- park where there are other people around whenever possible;
- use only well lit car parks at night.

When you park your car:

- leave it where it will be safe;
- take valuables with you whenever this is practicable;
- lock anything else in the boot or cover it up;
- do not leave children unattended in a car – they may release the handbrake;
- kidnapping is happening more frequently – do not leave babies in a car unless you are keeping sight of it;
- make sure all the windows and doors are properly closed and locked;
- if you are leaving a pet in the car, leave a window slightly open. Your car will be more secure if you put a grille in the space. Animals, however, should not be left in cars for long periods in hot weather;
- if your car is fitted with an alarm make sure it is working properly.

If you see anyone hanging around parked vehicles suspiciously, inform the police.

By following the above advice, and putting into practice the routines and procedures described in this and Section 5 of this book, I hope your driving in the future becomes even more enjoyable.

7 Advanced Driving Tests and Training

This section describes the different types of advanced driving tests which are available to the experienced motorist. It also covers the requirements of the Approved Driving Instructor Register should you wish to develop the skills of new drivers and improve the standards of driving on our roads.

Independent assessment of your personal driving skills

Should you wish to take any of the advanced tests, it may be useful to have your driving independently assessed. The various examining bodies each look for slight differences in style of driving and you will need to be aware of them.

Because of the pass or fail element involved, many experienced drivers shy away from driving tests. However, you may find it extremely interesting just to have your driving assessed. You may even find that the information given will enhance your style of driving and improve your running costs. The author, Margaret Stacey, operates a training establishment in Derbyshire to which independent drivers travel from all parts of the country.

In-house assessments can be organised for fleet operators. Company drivers' skills are assessed and weaknesses identified. Reports are then prepared for submission to the company's insurance broker, showing that steps are being taken to reduce the risk of accident involvement. Results in the past have proved successful with reduced insurance premiums being achieved.

For more information write to:

Margaret Stacey
AUTODRIVA
The Mount
53 Heanor Road
Ilkeston
Derbyshire DE7 8DY

The College of Driver Education (CODE)

This relatively new charitable organisation has been set up with four major aims:

- to help raise the general standard of driving;
- to ensure that driving instructors are thoroughly trained;
- to assist in funding and developing research into driving matters;
- to provide a counselling service to victims of road accidents.

The College is under the direction of a small number of trustees, who are dedicated, unsalaried people from all walks of life. All have an interest in driving, training and traffic affairs, as well as human relations.

CODE has appointed a number of assessors located throughout the country who will give an honest assessment of your driving and offer constructive advice on how to improve your skills. Because there is no 'pass or fail' element, you may feel this idea is much more acceptable than taking a test.

The assessment drive, taken in your own vehicle, will last for approximately 45 minutes, followed by an appraisal of your skills. The resultant benefits of taking a CODE assessment are:

- reduced insurance premiums (CODE has negotiated this with various companies);
- improved driving performance making your motoring more enjoyable and economical;
- updating your knowledge of rules, regulations and procedures;
- improving your confidence to prepare you for an advanced test.

If you require more information, or would like to apply for an assessment with CODE, write to:

The Secretary
The College of Driver Education
234 Tottenhall Road
Palmers Green
London N13 6DE

The Institute of Advanced Motorists (IAM)

The Institute was founded in 1956 by motorists from all walks of life with the common aim of making our roads safer by raising driving standards. It is controlled by a council elected for its members' expertise in various spheres of motoring.

The IAM motto is 'Skill with Responsibility' and it has over 250,000 members who have passed the test. An 'Advanced Motorist':

- is an above-average driver;
- concentrates all the time they are at the wheel;
- has complete control of the car at all times and in all circumstances, i.e. is in the correct part of the road, has the correct gear engaged and is travelling at the correct speed;
- drives safely and with courtesy;
- sets a good example to others.

You may consider taking the IAM test to satisfy yourself that you have a high standard of driving and are doing everything you can to promote road safety. Although approximately 60 per cent of candidates pass this test at the first attempt, with many of those failing pass at the second, should you fail, it will have no effect on the validity of your driving licence.

The IAM test is designed by the council of the Institute to incorporate a system of planned driving. It lasts about one and a half hours in order to give you time to settle down and drive in your normal manner.

The examiners hold the highest driving qualifications available, and receive special training in the art of assessment to ensure consistency in marking candidates.

During the test
The following aspects of your driving will be assessed:

- *acceleration* – this should be smooth and progressive. It should be used at the right time in the right place, with the correct amount of pressure being applied;
- *braking* – should also be smooth and progressive. Brakes should be used after mirrors have been checked. You should take into account the road and traffic conditions and brake early and gently;
- *clutch control* – the engine and road speeds must be properly co-ordinated when changing gear. You should not slip or ride the clutch, or coast with the clutch disengaged;
- *gear changing* – gears should be selected smoothly and fluently. If you are using an automatic car, make full and efficient use of it;
- *use of gears* – use the gears correctly. The right gear should be selected before reaching a hazard;
- *steering* – hold the wheel correctly with your hands at the quarter to three or ten to two position. Crossing your arms, except when manoeuvring in a confined space, is not recommended by the Institute;
- *seating position* – you should be alert and not slumped at the wheel. Do not rest an arm on the door when you are driving;
- *observation* – you should read the road well ahead, anticipating the actions of other road users. You should be able to correctly judge the speeds and distances of other vehicles;
- *concentration* – concentrate on the road and traffic situation – do not allow yourself to be distracted;
- *maintaining progress* – make good use of your vehicle's performance by driving at a reasonable pace, maintaining good progress throughout, but taking into consideration the road, traffic and weather conditions;
- *obstruction* – do not obstruct other road users by driving too slowly, by positioning incorrectly or by failing to anticipate and react correctly to the traffic situation ahead;
- *positioning* – you should always be in the correct part of the road, especially when approaching and negotiating hazards;
- *lane discipline* – drive in the appropriate lane and be careful not to straddle white lines;
- *observation of surfaces* – continually assess the road surface, especially in poor weather, and look out for slippery conditions;
- *traffic signals* – you should observe and respond correctly to signals, signs and road markings and extend proper courtesies at pedestrian crossings;
- *speed limits and other legal requirements* – these must be observed at all times;

- *overtaking* – overtake safely, maintaining a correct distance from other vehicles, using the mirrors, signals and gears correctly;
- *hazard procedure and cornering* – you must have full control over your vehicle on the approach to hazards, negotiating them in the correct position and driving at an appropriate speed with a suitable gear engaged;
- *mirrors* – use all of your mirrors frequently, especially before signalling or changing your speed or course;
- *signals* – these should be used where necessary. Use the direction indicator, or arm signals if required, in good time and at the right place. The horn and headlight flasher should only be used in accordance with the Highway Code;
- *restraint* – you should display reasonable restraint, without being indecisive;
- *consideration* – show consideration and courtesy to other road users;
- *vehicle sympathy* – do not over-stress your vehicle, for example by revving the engine needlessly or by braking fiercely;
- *manoeuvres* – these should be carried out smoothly and competently.

When you pass the IAM Test you may:

- display the Institute's badge on your car;
- take advantage of special insurance terms;
- receive *Milestones*, the IAM's own motoring magazine;
- join the local IAM group and participate in the road safety, driving and social events which they organise.

Further information and application forms for this test can be obtained from:

The Institute of Advanced Motorists
IAM House
359 Chiswick High Road
London W4 4HS
Tel: 0181-994 4403   Fax: 0181-994 9249

The Royal Society for the Prevention of Accidents (RoSPA) Advanced Driving Test

Tests are conducted at locations all over the UK by RoSPA's examiners who are all police Class 1 drivers. The test lasts for at least one and a quarter hours and covers a wide variety of road and traffic conditions.

This test is of a very high standard and RoSPA have a unique system of grading successful candidates into three categories:

- Gold;
- Silver;
- Bronze.

If you decide to take this test, you are recommended to read the police drivers' manual: *Roadcraft*. You are unlikely to achieve the highest grade if you don't have a good knowledge of the system of driving it recommends.

The test

The examiner will try to put you at your ease at the beginning of the test. Try to relax and drive as you would normally. Remember to carry out the correct 'cockpit drill' and a running brake test as you set off.

Your use of the controls:

- *steering:* the positioning of your hands and arms and use of the wheel will be assessed – try not to cross your hands;
- *clutch:* use it smoothly and gently. Your examiner will be pleased to see double declutching where appropriate. Do not slip or ride the clutch;
- *gears:* should be engaged smoothly and the engine revolutions matched correctly to the road speed. The correct timing of gear changes will be assessed;
  - the use of intermediate gears when appropriate may affect your final grading;
  - the use of 'hold' or 'kickdown' on the automatic box will be noted;
- *brakes:* your smooth and early braking in accordance with the 'system of car control' will be noted. Skid avoidance and a 'tapering' of the pressure will be expected to bring the vehicle to smooth stops without any jerkiness;
- *accelerator:* use it firmly when needed and precisely and under control at all times. Exercise accelerator sense to vary the speed of the car to meet changing conditions without braking, and apply power in the right quantity at all times;
- *the 'system':* you will be expected to apply this in the correct sequence at all times and keep up to date with what is happening to the rear. Over-the-shoulder looks are required at the appropriate times;
- *horn:* whether you use this when necessary and in the correct manner;
- *visibility:* keep your windows clear at all times using the wipers, demisters or an open window if necessary.

Driving performance:

- *moving off and stopping:* this should be carried out smoothly and precisely applying the necessary safety measures;
- *show that you understand the 'system':* ensure that your actions are carried out in the correct sequence. For example, make sure your braking is completed before you make a gear change;
- *positioning:* your car should be positioned correctly at all times on the approach to all hazards;
- *cornering:* positioning is important both in town and at maximum speed on the open road. The line you take should give you maximum vision and safety margin;
- *signalling:* signals should be used when necessary and timed correctly. Do not use unnecessary signals but where appropriate arm signals should be used. Act promptly on traffic signs and markings;
- *reversing:* this should be carried out competently, precisely and safely;
- *making progress:* you should drive up to the maximum legal limits wherever safe;
- *overtaking:* should be efficiently carried out when safe, legal and necessary.

General ability:

- your alertness will be considered – sit properly at the controls and do not rest your elbows;
- your consideration for other road users and self-discipline will be assessed. Your temperament should remain calm and relaxed while driving;
- you should show respect for your vehicle, driving with sympathy for it at all times;
- how far ahead you are planning and anticipating will demonstrate your experience and ability;
- your judgement of speed and distance of your own and other vehicles will be noted;
- in heavy traffic, your anticipation of what is happening to vehicles well ahead of the one in front will be assessed and it may be useful to give a commentary to demonstrate how far ahead you are planning;
- your knowledge of the Highway Code and basic car mechanics will be tested at the end of the drive. It may also be useful to read your vehicle's handbook.

At the end of the test:

- The examiner will discuss any points which may have arisen during your drive. You will be told whether you have passed and, if so, what grade you have achieved. This will be followed up in four to six weeks by a typed report and you will also receive a signed certificate.
- If you achieve a Gold or Silver pass you will be expected to take a refresher test at subsequent three-year intervals. If you achieve a Bronze grading, you must take a test once a year until a higher grade is achieved. If you fail, you will be permitted to take a re-test after three months. Guidance will be offered.
- If your grading is below Gold, it is suggested that you join a local group, where other members will be able to offer advice.

The benefits of membership

When you are accepted as a member of the RoSPA Advanced Drivers Association you have to undertake to:

- do everything possible to further its ideals amongst other road users;
- remember that all people have equal rights on the road;
- display the Association Badge with pride and maintain the Association's high standards;
- maintain your vehicle in a roadworthy condition;
- adopt the Highway Code as the guide to good behaviour on the road;
- take a regular refresher test.

Applying for the test

For further information or an application form apply to:

The Administrative Officer
RoSPA Advanced Drivers Association
Cannon House
The Priory Queensway
Birmingham B4 6BS

The Cardington special driving test for driving instructors

If you are a driving instructor and have not had your driving assessed or tested for some time, you may be interested in this special driving test which is conducted at the Driving Standards Agency's (DSA) Training Establishment at Cardington in Bedfordshire.

To be able to cope with today's changing road and traffic conditions, it is extremely important that your pupils are taught to drive to the latest efficient methods. You may find it extremely informative to take a refresher course with a tutor to make sure your personal driving skills meet the DSA's current high standards.

The test:

- lasts for about an hour and a half;
- is conducted in your own vehicle, which must have a manual gearbox;
- covers a wide range of road and traffic situations.

The examiner will be assessing:

- whether you handle the car efficiently and sympathetically;
- how you apply the MSM – PSL – LADA routines;
- your planning and approach to all hazards;
- whether you make positive progress at all times, taking into consideration the road and traffic conditions;
- whether you are courteous and considerate to other road users, and can correctly anticipate their actions.

There is no theory element to this test and you will not be expected to give a commentary while you are driving.

The standard required to pass this test is extremely high. If you make more than two minor or one serious error you will fail. You will not be told of the result immediately as the examiner will have to discuss his report with the Chief Instructor before a grading can be given. You will normally be notified of the result within forty-eight hours.

If you receive a grade 'A' you will be eligible to receive the Cardington 'Special Test Certificate'.

Courses in high performance handling techniques

If you are interested in extending your driving skills and would like to attend training in skid control or high performance techniques, there are various centres throughout the UK. These include:

Ecosse Driving
Skid Control Training
29 Cavendish Close
Castle Donnington
Leicestershire

High Performance Course Ltd
Unit 10, Seven House
Town End
Caterham
Surrey CR3 5UG

RallyDrive
153 High Street
Hull HU1 1PA

The Register of Approved Driving Instructors

If you have a keen interest in improving the standards of driving on our roads and are also looking for a change in career, driving instruction offers lots of job satisfaction.

However, you should bear in mind that it is not an easy job. Because you are a good driver does not necessarily mean you will make a good instructor. Before signing up on courses and paying out lots of money in advance, you should consider the following:

- the ADI examination is very stringent;
- you will need lots of expert training;
- you need patience, concentration and stamina;
- you have to deal with people from all walks of life;
- you have to work unsociable hours which may sometimes affect your family life;
- your car will sometimes be abused.

The driving instruction market is undergoing many changes:

- because of the falling birthrate, there is a decline in the numbers of seventeen year olds;
- the middle-aged market has almost disappeared;
- you will have to learn how to teach the theoretical elements involved in driving to prepare pupils for the new test;
- you will have to be positive about finding different markets.

The ADI Examination
The examination to qualify as an Approved Driving Instructor is conducted in three parts and they have to be taken and passed in the following sequence:

- *Part 1 – Test of Theory:* a paper of 100 multiple-choice questions. The examination is banded into four sections and, to pass, you must score a minimum of 80 per cent in each of these, and attain an overall pass mark of 85 per cent.
- *Part 2 – Test of Driving Ability:* a driving test of about an hour's duration. Your driving will be assessed on all types of roads and the test includes:
  - a left- and right-hand reverse;
  - a turn in the road exercise;
  - a reverse parking exercise;
  - an emergency stop, which could be given at well over 30 mph.

The standard required to pass is extremely high. If you accumulate six or more minor errors, or one serious or dangerous one, you will fail.

- *Part 3 – Test of Instructional Ability:* a test of an hour's duration in which your teaching skills will be assessed at two different levels:
  - *Phase 1:* the examiner will role play a learner with very little experience and you will have to assess the teaching level required;
  - *Phase 2:* the examiner will role play an 'experienced' learner who is about at driving test standard and you will have to assess the standard, identify errors and make suggestions for improvement.

Further information about the ADI Register is available in a special brochure called *The ADI.14 – Your Road to Becoming an Approved Driving Instructor.* This is available for £2.50 from:

The ADI Register
Driving Standards Agency
Stanley House
Talbot Street
Nottingham NG1 5GU

For information on training for the examination contact the author:

Margaret Stacey
AUTODRIVA
The Mount
53 Heanor Road
Ilkeston
Derbyshire DE7 8DY

Conclusion

The main aim of this book is to help improve the hazard awareness of motorists with a keen interest in driving, like yourself. I hope you have found it interesting and that your driving becomes even more enjoyable and relaxed. You might even encourage your friends to read it and perhaps get them to join you in taking one of the advanced tests. After all, we have to share our roads, not only with new, inexperienced drivers, but also with lots of people who have been driving for many years. If we can get them to improve their own personal skills, the roads will be safer for everyone.